War! Politics! And the

Human Comedy!

Scenes and

Monologues

W. Colin McKay

ISBN: 0988460807
ISBN-13: 9780988460805

DEDICATION

FOR

My wife, my love, CARY

Who is my inspiration, my muse, my biggest supporter, my beta-reader, and without a doubt, my permission-giver to write, and, therefore, to bother others with my theatrically encased comments and observations on the human comedy we call Life.

To the four key figures in my life, plus two:

My dad, Wallie, who always had faith I'd live to tell the tale, and my mother, Olive, who was convinced I'd end up dying alone in a dark alley. Who knows? There's still time.

My sons, Kirk and Conan (identical twins who separately taught me how to love unconditionally and continue to teach me daily) -- without them there'd be an infinite vacuum, plus there would be no granddaughters, all of whom I love beyond measure.

and

To Dorothe Bonsignore, who saved this fifteen-year-old kid from wandering off into oblivion and whose support sparked a fire still burning. She was the sole reason high school was not just a place to escape.

To Dr. William (Bill) Adams, whose encouragement guided me, and kept the fire fed, and protected me from the fire extinguisher of higher education. He provided my first glimpse of a creative home.

CONTENTS

CONTENTS (CON'T)

CONTENTS (Con't)

W. Colin McKay

ACKNOWLEDGMENTS

When you've been around for as long as I have and done so many things, you accumulate an incredibly long list of people who contributed to your longevity. For me, they are legion. I know this. Please accept my apologies to anyone I fail to mention. You are all crucial to my story.

"People ask me when I decided to become a playwright, and I tell them I decide to do it every day. Most days ... when I sit down to write, I can't remember how it's done."
Suzan Lori-Parks

From San Diego State College my close and respected friends, who trusted my stage direction and my writings enough to allow me to trust myself; Sheldon Gero (who also taught me to play chess); Cleavon Little (I wrote, Cleavon starred in, and together, we produced the first play at San Diego City College Black History Month. We shared the death threats with both humor and vigilance); Bill Poschman; Ginger Brubeck (fellow actor since high school); Fred Berling; Roland McFarland; Janet Mitchell; Gabby Winzurk; and James Jones.

Oakland Children's Theatre Program where, as director and playwright, I cut my teeth on audiences who gave *immediate* reaction to what occurred on stage. I learned things like evil dragons should not exit through an audience determined to defeat them. I also appreciated the depth of artistic accomplishment, and the universality of human emotions demonstrated by the young actors: especially Paula Anderson, the sisters Lynne, Lora, and Lisa Thielbar, and Gloria Luffendahl (who's artistic sensibilities far outreached her young age). A special debt of gratitude goes to Robert (Bob) Hudson, great director, teacher, colleague, collaborator on the only musical I've ever written, and a great human being.

One name stands out for me in Philadelphia -- Sara Garonzik, Executive Producing Director, Emeritus -- the force and genius who steered the Philadelphia Theatre Company to new heights nationwide. Sara gifted me with one of my most satisfying moments in playwriting when The Philadelphia Theatre Company produced the premiere of *Nagasaki Dust*. During rehearsals I felt something was missing. I carried it around like a heavy rock chained to my feet. When I mentioned the dilemma to Sara, she cocked her head and said, "Maybe if your two male leads were to have a scene where they talked to each other about something other than the trial, there might be something there." Needless to say there was, and I passed that new scene to the director and actors at the next rehearsal. It became a key scene of the play. Thank you, Sara. And, thank you to the outstanding actors of this production Yuji Okumoto, Tim Guinee, Tamlyn Tomita, Alan Feinstein, Greg Edelman, James Saito, Jay Patterson, and my director of this play, Jules Aaron.

I took root and called East Los Angeles College my home base, where I served as Director of Theatre. My thanks to my staff, who made it an outstanding place to continue learning about and participating in the theatrical experience: Jim Ishida (who also became my collaborator on the play *Nagasaki Dust*), Tom Atha, Bob Delagall, Kelley Hogan, David Laird Scott, Glen Chin, Bill Shick, Michael (Kaz) Kaznetsis, Laura McLane, Jim Buglewicz, Vanessa Mizzone, Ken Plum, Rodney Scott, Dan Keleher, and all the staff members who held it together. Among all of us we had an extraordinarily professional team assembled, representing industry unions and guilds. It was a remarkable time with remarkable students, many of whom are currently theatre professionals: Cecilia Garcia, Peter Mendoza, Sebastian Fernandez, Alex Jimenez, Ron Trejo, Marianne Fritz, Ray Quiroga, and Jose Garcia. I'm proud of them, of course, but just as proud of those who pursued other careers in education, music, and communication.

Blue Sphere Alliance, a professional acting company based in Hollywood where it was an exciting place filled with young professionals who all loved theatre. The executive director, mover, and shaker, Anthony Barnao, kept the company vision and created a first-rate theatre company, where it was a joy to work as Resident Playwright, Dramaturge, and Literary Manager. Among the many others in this company were Kim Tobin, Christian Campbell, Steve Johnson, Jonelle Allen, Alyson Croft and Sandra Thigpen.

Theater East was driven by its leaders Anita Khasadian, Alan Naggar, Christopher White, and the irreplaceable Peter Haskell. This professional theatre company served as the home for many of my plays. They are a highly professional group and a delight to direct. I consider myself very lucky to have served as co-chair of the Writer's Unit with Anita Khanzadian, an outstanding director, superb actress (I say that objectively, as I directed her in several shows), and, most of all, a marvelous person.

I had a great time working with Actor's Studio West –Writers Unit. What an exceptional group. Many nights I walked away inspired and thrilled to have spent the evening, discussing the craft of playwriting with a fabulous group of playwrights. Of course, Martin Landau and Mark Rydell offered excellent critiques. I remember one night when Mark spotted a thread running through one of my plays that had been overlooked by everyone else and assured me (much to my sense of encouragement) a professional director or actor would find it in rehearsal and be excited by its potential. It was here I felt the immense impact of Elaine Madsen, who invited me into the unit and whose faith in my work was affirming.

There is another individual I want to mention. His impact on me and his insightful comments on my work has been significant: Anthony (Tony) Massucci, FTM Productions. Tony hung in there with me and had my back when the going got tough. I value his friendship.

Finally, I'd liked to acknowledge all the theatre professionals onstage and off, in the scenes or behind the scenes, whose excellence made my plays work so well in production, and to all the students who passed my way and, in return, taught me. All of you helped make me the writer I am. My sincere thanks and gratitude.

W. Colin McKay

Introduction

Elephant in the Room

When all the hullabaloo and commotion accompanying this book dies down and all the noise is replaced with quiet, it will be the time for the elephant in the room to squirm about, lift his trunk and growl (yes, elephant's growl).

To an outsider it might appear the elephant is asking for nothing more than a plate of peanuts. To the insider, me, the elephant is not asking for peanuts, but, instead, the elephant is asking, "What on earth is there about this book that would lead anyone in their right mind to buy it, use it, and share it with a friend?" Good question, elephant, let me tell you. The bits and pieces you find here have had successful lives in larger productions with the characters developed in a variety of ways by each individual actor.

There is implicit in the question of how I, the playwright, develop characters on the page. The complete answer is long and involved with my everyday work of writing (that's why I conduct workshops), but there is a quick answer. When developing characters, I look to the societal rules framing their lives. That's it, in a peanut shell. Every person lives by societal rules often so rigid as to determine details of their lives like who they can marry and how to live, they must learn the behavior in a given society or be prepared live as a societal outlaw. My job as the playwright is to discover the success of any character at staying within those rules, and to show how they feel about their lives within those social constraints.

What does this book offer you? Each monologue, each scene is complete unto itself. They have been extracted from another, larger source, and placed on these pages. You are performing a small, independent chunk of a larger piece. Consequently, how you approach this smaller piece is up to you. You may determine a whole new set of rules with little or no resemblance to the larger piece. This is your chance to create your own universe.

It is assumed that these monologues and scenes will be used primarily for auditions or forensic competitions. Keeping that in mind, you are still exploring the rules of character. With that said, let me encourage you to also explore changing the rules of gender, race or other diversities. And why not? For example, the monologue "Killed by Shadows" is set in a jungle. There is no reference to time or specific jungle and there is no reference to gender. To me, it's perfectly clear a female or a person of any racial or cultural background could perform the monologue "Killed by Shadows." Please make it yours.

It is my hope you will find the material contained within the pages of this small book to be challenging and empowering, allowing your talent to shine a little brighter in audition or performance. In all, I wish you well and give you full permission to approach the material as you will. However, in the interest of honoring the craft of a playwright please don't rewrite more than a few words if adapting these offerings. Always remember, there's more than meets the eye. If you have questions on the material contained in this book, or after using the material you have comments, please contact me at: mckay01@gmail.com.

CHAPTER ONE

MONOLOGUES FOR WOMEN

W. Colin McKay

DONE WITH IT

From the one-act comedy, *Tables*

By W. Colin McKay

BACKGROUND: "Tables" is a one-act comedy serially connected by separate scenes, each following from the other.
SETTING: Outside a bus terminal. There's the sound of buses.
SCENE: DIANE is answering Fred, her husband, who asked if she'd give him a divorce?

DIANE

Yes. I'd give it to you easily, with no protracted lawyer fights. And then, Fred...I'd shoot you. I've put a great deal of time and effort into making this marriage work. I've gone out of my way to listen to you, whenever you've chosen to talk, although, to be honest, for the most part, I find your conversation dull and unimportant.

I've attempted to make an attractive home, even though last week you referred to it as both stifling and unappealing. By the way, in case you haven't noticed, I have since redone the colors of the front room. I've made myself accessible to you sexually. Not enough for you, I suspect, but certainly within reason. I even said yes to the handcuffs and blindfold. In short, I have tried and continue to try to cater to you and to make sure you are comfortable in the marriage. I plan, prepare, anticipate to the best of my ability to ensure a good marriage, a pleasant life.

For you to throw away all my work would not suit me. I would rather kill you.

Age: Mid 40s Late 30s

Body type: full, a little plumpy not too much

wearing: purple blouse
Gold hoops
(a brunette)

*Not a gay marriage

HANDLE IT

From the full-length drama, *Zone of Separation*

By W. Colin McKay

BACKGROUND: STEPHANIE is girlfriend to Toni Prentice, a female Army veteran who served four top-secret deployments in Afghanistan only to be sent home battling for her sanity.

SETTING: Apartment of Toni and STEPHANIE.

SCENE: STEPHANIE is explaining how she feels about Toni.

STEPHANIE

Damn it, stop trying to be funny. Listen to me.

(pause)

Thanks.

(pauses)

Sweetie, my last two relationships were wound up cannons, like you. One of them was a guy. Whether they were male or female, when things blew up and went this side of crazy, both of my ex-partners said they could "handle it". My boyfriend "handled it" by beating the crap out of me. My girlfriend "handled it" by holding a gun on me for six hours.

I know you'd never hurt me. I don't want you to think I'm saying that.

God, honey, when you touch me…I've never been touched the way you touch me. I've never had anyone be so soft and…careful. You touch me like you're…appreciative. *hugging stroking (petting)*

(takes a breath)

I know things happened to you in Afghanistan. At night, when you're asleep lying next to me, I can feel you shaking. Your body fighting with itself. Trying to push away whatever it is that happened. And I'm not sure if you're winning. It scares me when you say you can "take care of yourself." You know, suicide is just another way of "taking care of yourself." Toni, my dearest love, I'm a waitress in a dive, happy when a patron actually leaves a tip. I mean, I don't need a lot. You've given me everything I need. It scares me. I could be–have been–called a "loser." I don't want to keep proving it, you know? … Being with you, having you love me, proves … I'm no loser.

Body type: thin, fragile
time of day: Late, maybe approaching or passing midnight

BABY CRIES

From the full-length drama, *Children of Shame*

By W. Colin McKay

BACKGROUND: During the Bosnia-Serbia conflict, MOLLY HINSON is working as a contract investigator for the U.N. War Tribunal. Her boss, Captain Frank Morgan, USN, wants her to interview a Christian missionary who works in the middle of Bosnia and who supposedly has photographic evidence of war crimes committed by a high-ranking Serbian military officer. MOLLY wants to go home on leave but is being talked into staying for the one investigation. The most significant problem is that the missionary in question is a brigadier in the Christian Missionary Army, and MOLLY despises missionaries in general, but, specifically those in the Christian Missionary Army.

SETTING: Bare stage except for MOLLY.

SCENE: MOLLY delivers the opening monologue. It is retrospective in nature, distanced from any simultaneous action onstage.

MOLLY

The last time I saw her she told me about her recurring "baby dream". She'd find herself standing in the middle of a large, infinite room carpeted with babies, filled with their noise. It was deafening. Yet, at the far end, beyond sight, cutting through the overwhelming uproar, she could hear the anguished cry of a baby in great pain. She'd start toward it, but there were so many babies that every step she made had to be slow, carefully executed so as not to step on another baby. The cry would grow louder, more demanding. She'd try to hurry, but the other babies kept shifting, twisting, rolling into her path forcing her to step sideways, then back, then forward, sideways, back, turn, step. Suddenly, she realized with all her attempts to get to the baby, she'd returned to where she began. The baby's wail became louder, more persistent.

It was the desperate cry of a baby dying. She hesitated and then ran, stepping on the twisting bodies as lightly as possible, hoping against hope not to add to their pain. But it was futile. With every step, no matter how hesitant, she could feel her feet crushing, snapping fragile bones. But she kept running. With every step another agonized shriek. With every step, a grinding of a small arm or leg or hand. Babies screaming. Their suffering sounding out over each other, louder and louder, then abruptly -- she realized she couldn't hear the first baby's cry over the tormented pandemonium.

She stopped. Frozen. Wanting to reach out to that one infant. Knowing somewhere a baby had died a terrible death, knowing she had caused the very turmoil, which prevented her from bringing relief -- in her dream -- she stood there, sobbing, believing...knowing, she had failed.

PATTERNS ON PATTERNS

From the one-act comedy, *Time After Time*

By W. Colin McKay

BACKGROUND: This play is a farcical, non-linear exploration of relationships which serve as stumbling blocks to personal goals.

SETTING: A bare stage, with actors entering and exiting from non-specific areas, addressing the audience in the middle of a scene, and moving in and out of the onstage light.

SCENE: GRETCHEN, arrogant and proud is explaining to her husband, Joe, how she plans and approaches life.

GRETCHEN

I earned my B.A. from Princeton in Forensic Accounting. That degree allowed me to scrutinize numbers to see the crime. And that's what I did. With the numbers thus scrutinized, I astutely identified employee theft, penetrated the rungs of securities fraud. Oh God, what fun it was. All numbers were exposed. Trapped. I had caught them cold, hung them out, and sprinkled their ashes in space. I, Gretchen Holigophy, used numbers to, poof, make the invisible visible and, thus, reveal insurance hocus pocus.

Damn it, Joe, listen to me. Try to understand. With my B.A. no number escaped me. I was ready to grow more powerful. My M.A. from Stanford. One year. My project was published. A scholarly article. "Financial Statement Analysis". My name on it. Nobody else's name. My name. Only my name. On an important article. Do you know what that demonstrated? Do you, Joe? It demonstrated I not only knew how to scrutinize numbers. I now knew what numbers meant. How they could be used for more than solving crime. I now knew how to corner them, grab them, hold them up for study one by one, then pin them on paper and watch them wriggle. Like captured butterflies pinned on a wall.

Then came my doctorate. Yale. Data Analytics. Synthesizing the numbers I'd caught and held prisoner. Putting them under the glare of the immense blinding light of my mind, interrogating them, forcing them to uncover patterns, reveal relationships to those patterns, in those patterns, and, most important, to tell me what trends those patterns predicted. "Predictive Data Analytics!" A book. An important book. A very important book. About what? About what? Oh, Joe, Joe, Joe. What's going to happen tomorrow, that's what!! Knowing when things will start! Knowing… when… things… will… end. My mind discovered, well, a more accurate word would be, uncovered, the underbelly of statistics. I discovered the never-before-uncovered relationship of statistics to the universe. My analysis revealed the ebb and flow of fate. Joe, don't you see?

Statistics frame the template of life. For every statistical pattern there's a numerical reaction...to Time. I'm channeling Time! Do you understand? Joe, do you understand? Of course, you don't! Can't! You poor sap! You drink beer, watch television, live a life with no statistical knowledge of it's numerical stature on the grid of existence! While, I!... Me!... I!... have Time at my fingertips, gaily cavorting in the vineyard of my mind, hippity-hop, hippity-hop, hop, hop, hop, while you let eternity flounder, hopelessly entangled in the marshmallow morass of your intellect, of which I believe there is nothing left to see, touch, or... feed... to the cat.

TWISTED BABIES

From the full-length play, *Fallujah*
By W. Colin McKay

BACKGROUND: The play takes place after the Battle for Fallujah, 2004 and explores relationships and lives of soldiers during an investigation of the suspicious deaths of three soldiers supposedly killed by friendly fire.
SETTING: A bare stage except for the field medic.
SCENE: A U.S. ARMY FIELD MEDIC addresses the audience.

FEMALE FIELD MEDIC

I'd been a pediatrician back home. Over here, I work mostly with Muslim mothers whose husbands are missing... either killed or imprisoned. In this society, a single woman and child, alone for whatever reason, is extremely vulnerable. If something goes wrong, her baby is sick or hurt and the woman has little or no money, she's in a desperate situation.

There are no jobs to be had ... for women. Consequently, to make money, many find the only solution is selling their bodies. Once they do that, they are isolated and made more alone. Then the women kept getting pregnant. And to care for their children they need money. It's a vicious cycle. That's why there are so many prostitutes in Iraq. We try to help them, but it has become more and more difficult. With so many wounded in Fallujah, there's minimal aid available for them and their children.

And minimal aid is not going to be enough to help with deformed babies. And I believe it's our fault they're deformed. When I first began encountering these babies, I thought it an anomaly. However, I checked Basra. The number of deformed babies reported exceeded the norm. Ramadi reported the same. Wherever I looked, the problem kept growing.

It seemed out of proportion to anywhere near normal. I didn't know what to make of it. How could there be so many? What's causing it? I thought finding the reason would be hard. I was wrong. It didn't take much research. Depleted Uranium. The deformed babies had been born to mothers whose bodies were contaminated with extreme toxic radiation levels.

(pauses)

The U.S. uses depleted uranium as a covering for our weaponry. It blows the hell out of people on the ground . . . and then leaves radiation behind to kill the survivors, or those who thought they survived.

The military denies there's a problem even though we've already dumped the equivalent of 250,000 times the nuclear waste that was dumped on Nagasaki. Of course, it doesn't do it's damage or kill or maim right away. It takes it time. These twisted babies are the result of the first Gulf War. This war will take its time, too. The women who are not yet impregnated have no idea what they'll be giving to their babies when they do become pregnant. Those babies will be trapped inside a body that'll be feeding their hearts, their lungs, their brains, daily doses of toxic waste.

The hell of it is, we wanted to start a family when I got home. How in the hell am I going to tell my husband that I'm afraid of what we'll have? I've been here over a year. Being a medic, I'm always in the middle of things. Always surrounded by radiation. Even if my kids are born all right, who knows how long they'll go before they get cancer, or leukemia, or God knows what?

This is a toxic swamp over here and it isn't going away. Every soldier, every civilian, every ally, every damn person over here gets hit. Christ, what do I tell my husband? . . . How do I tell him?

FLUSH HIM DOWN

From the full-length dark comedy, *Where Nobody Belongs*
By W. Colin McKay

BACKGROUND: Red is an alcoholic do-nothing. His daughter, SUE, is trying to escape the family, but wants to bring her abused mother with her.

SETTING: Living room of modest, lower class home.

SCENE: SUE is trying to get her mother to understand it's not her fault Red hit her.

SUE

Damn it, it's not your fault he hit you. And it's not your fault he got fired. They fired him at the warehouse because he showed up drunk. They had warned him, twice, for Christ's sake, and he still did it again. It's not your fault they fired him and it's definitely, definitely, not your fault he hit you. The son-of-a-bitch hit you because you wouldn't give him any money. Money you worked for and he didn't. Telling him no was the only answer. You did the right thing. Well, thinking about it, maybe not. Maybe you didn't do the right thing. Maybe the right thing would've been to snuff him out.

       (beat)

Mom, I'm sorry. You know I am. But I've told you a hundred times what to do. Leave the bastard. We can make it on our own. My God, we're making it on our own now. I work nights. You hold two jobs. All to support him. He only does two things. Drink and get fired. All that crap he spouts that he drinks because of the accident is bullshit. He had the accident because he was drunk. Too bad it was just his arm got cut. His throat would've been better. Mom, you're married to a piece of shit and I'm sure God'll forgive you if you flush him down the toilet.

A SAFE PLACE

From the full-length drama, *Children of Shame*
By W. Colin McKay

BACKGROUND: SISTER DENIS is a Christian Missionary working in Serbia during the Serbia-Bosnia conflict. She is one of three missionaries being interviewed by Molly Hinson, an U.N. War Crimes Tribunal investigator. Because Molly is searching for evidence of war crimes, she is trying to scare the missionaries by acting tough and out-of-control. While the other missionaries have continued to be polite and caring in the face of Molly's behavior. Sister Denis is breaking form.

SETTING: Work room in the mission.

SCENE: Molly has been acting tough, swearing at the missionaries, trying to push them around.

SISTER DENIS

Oh, shut up! Don't you get it? How dumb are you? The Serbs captured these women. Imprisoned them. Raped them in their cells. Daily. Over and over, until they became pregnant with Serbian babies. These women have had their identities, their lives, everyone they loved or who loved them, taken from them. They no longer have homes. Their families don't want them. Their husbands will murder them for allowing themselves to be raped. And, God help these women, they hate their babies. Those babies are children of shame. Eternal shame. These women are trapped in hell. They have no place to go.

This, this, what we have carved out for them on this little piece of Serbian soil, this! is all they have. Here! Without it they'd be at the mercy of the Serbian authorities and. . . well, you simply can't destroy what we're giving those women. To try to do so is immoral.

(pause)

It's wrong to come in here barking at everyone, acting like goddamn drunken fool. Oh, you flinched. You've been swearing at everyone, including poor Sister Bonnie. You dumb little girl. Sister Bonnie was captured by Muslims. She was raped and tortured. You swagger in swearing at her, bullying her. Jesus Christ, you poor thing, Sister Bonnie will be tougher than you when she's dead. Oh, and yes, you silly little girl, Sister Bonnie is actively serving and protecting Muslims. She's a true servant of the Lord. In case you don't get it, don't try pushing me around or you might be surprised how hard I can push back.

To hell with it! Ask your questions, and then get out. You're interfering with my work.

VANISHED

From the full-length drama, *Nagasaki Dust*

By W. Colin McKay

BACKGROUND: Inspired by a true story, Chuck Randolph is an Army lawyer directed to defend John Okui, a Japanese-American, being unfairly tried for treason by the United States Army.

SETTING: Courtroom.

SCENE: KIMIKO, has been called as witness and tells of the Atomic Bomb being dropped on Nagasaki.

KIMIKO

I thought my baby would be safe with his Auntie. They told me that Hiroshima had been destroyed. My whole family lived there. I had to go to them, to see if they were safe, but everyone kept talking about strange things in the air that hurt you and made you sick. So, I left my son, Bontaro, with Auntie and took the train to Hiroshima.

I didn't know what to expect. All the talk seemed crazy. I mean, a town doesn't just disappear. No bomb is that big. I prayed my family had found safety.

When I got to Hiroshima I knew they hadn't. The train rails stopped a few miles out of the city. Stopped. There were no more rails. I had to walk the rest of the way into the city. It was... very hard. Hiroshima was gone. The city had become a place of the dead. Wherever I looked, burned corpses.

I never found my family. Where we had lived no longer existed. I cried all day and said prayers. The next day I hurried back to my son, very early the morning of August ninth. He wasn't home when I arrived. Auntie had taken Bontaro with her to Our Lady of the Immaculate Conception to pray for the dead at Hiroshima. Before going to church, I helped distributed the warning flyers John had given me. After seeing Hiroshima, I thought the flyers would be useless if we were attacked. But I did it for John.

(beat)

I helped John even though I couldn't believe they would bomb Nagasaki. Compared to Hiroshima we were such an unimportant town. There were so many other bigger, more important towns. They certainly wouldn't drop such a terrible bomb here, I thought... That's what I thought.

(beat)

There had been five hundred people at mass, praying, when the bomb dropped directly on the church. Bontaro, Auntie, everyone ...they ... they all just vanished.

(pauses, then softly in anguish)

I didn't even wash his blanket.

WE GET OFF SCOT FREE

From the rom-com screenplay, *Crash Site*

By W. Colin McKay

BACKGROUND: "*Crash Site*" explores the legal machinations that occur after a train crash. Several of the lawyers, on all sides, are particularly cold-blooded, and aggressive. The corporate lawyers for the freight-hauling railroad in the screenplay lead the pack. HESTER is one of the most aggressive, "win at all costs" lawyers.

SETTING: Site of the injury incurred by three young teens, jumping a moving train with their bicycles.

SCENE: HESTER is explaining to George, a newly hired colleague, why the railroad she represents won't have to pay a dime for the horrific accident involving three young teens.

HESTER

Okay, George. Follow this. Three kids. They brought some shovels and dug a ramp. They built a landing area on the other side of the gully, and when the train came, they began jumping over it on their mountain bikes. Quite thrilling to be hurtling over a moving train. The first two made it. The third one missed and lost both legs. Cut off above the knee. That's terrible, of course, but he's going to live. The fire department got here in record time. As a consequence, here's how I see it legally. First, a cut fence is a misdemeanor. Second, trespassing, and defacement of property is another misdemeanor. Third, here's the big one, jumping a train and forcing it to stop to gather up legs and the rest of the body, thereby endangering the crew and any possible nearby individuals--a felony. If we're lucky on that one, we'll get two separate charges -- jumping the train, a felony, and the follow-up gathering of those parts of the body that missed the jump, another felony.

Please understand, I'm fully aware, the poor child got hurt. Losing legs is going to be expensive and, in normal circumstances, even though we could easily prove the mother should've had better control of her child and could demonstrate if she had been a better mother the accident wouldn't have happened in the first place, the court would order us to help with medical expenses. God, if, even in some small way, we were responsible ... like owning the train and the tracks ... the soft-hearted, liberal leaning court, would hit us with big numbers.

But, this time, we'll get off scot free. It's clear as a doorbell.
        (she pulls out a small book, quotes from it)
"The railroad is not liable for any accident which is the result of criminal activity."
        (quotes again)
"Not liable for any accident which is the result of criminal activity."
        (snaps book shut with joyous smile)
In other words, this "unfortunate event" is not going to cost us a dime. See how it works? Lucky me. . . I'm thinking a bonus.

THEY TRAPPED US

From the full-length drama, *Gentleman's War*

By W. Colin McKay

NOTE: *The play* <u>Gentleman's War</u> *is set in South Africa, 1900, during the South African War (Boer War). The South African War pitted the British Army against the Dutch Boers in a battle for geo-political supremacy of South Africa. It also served as the catalyst for the decades-long rule of Apartheid. COLONEL CLARK-HOWELLL is one of the main characters and is fashioned somewhat after Colonel Baden-Powell of Boy Scout fame. While the story is fictional, it is loosely based on Colonel Baden-Powell's experience as a commander during the actual Boer blockade of Mafeking, South Africa.*

BACKGROUND: The British have occupied a town by the name of Graysmith, but in so doing find themselves surrounded by Boers. The commanding officer is a delicate Colonel who sings and dances for the entertainment his troops and the town he governs. He praises his own ability as a scout and has a "special" relationship with one of his boys training to also be a scout. JEDEDIAH CARSON, an American reporter for a major San Francisco newspaper sent to observe the few Americans fighting for the Boers, is apprehended by British forces. The British suspect he may be a spy for the Boers. Jed is detained in Graysmith. The inhabitants of the occupied town are allowed to go about their daily business. One of the inhabitants is the widow, KATIE McKINNON, an East Indian who had been married to a British officer killed early in the conflict. She now runs a boarding house in Graysmith.

SETTING: A room in Katie McKinnon's boarding house.

SCENE: In spite of the personal danger to them, all dark-skinned females have been forced out of town by Colonel Clark-Howell, including KATIE McKINNON. She has escaped and returned to her lover, Jed.

KATIE

We never made it to the bush to hide. They saw Clark-Howell force the women out. As soon as we were out of range for help, the Boers trapped us. There were so many of them. It was. . . terrifying. We held hands to keep them out. They rode their horses into our bodies. Used their rifles as prods, tormenting us. All the women were screaming. The Boers just laughed and kept jabbing anyone who tried to run or fight. When they finally had us in a circle. . . they began. . . roping us. Pulling women out of the circle. The rope around our waists. Tight. Squeezing our lungs. Tripping our feet. Dragging us on the ground. Some of them making their horses charge at us. Then. . . then they came down on the ground. Choosing who to capture.

(tries to compose herself)

They began. . . tearing at our clothes. Ripping our blouses. Their fingernails scratched my skin making me bleed. I pleaded with them not to humiliate me, but they... Oh, Jed, it was horrible. After we were all naked, they began whipping us. They all had whips. Jed, it hurt. It hurt so much. I cried out, please. Please. They hit harder. . . One man tripped me with his whip. He began yelling that I wasn't like the others. I was lighter-skinned. More men came over and grabbed me. They held me down. They touched me. Poked me. One man said he'd never had a woman like me. Then another. . . Oh, Jedediah, how could they have been so cruel?

MY FAULT?

From the full-length drama, *Fallujah*
By W. Colin McKay

BACKGROUND: The play takes place after the Battle for Fallujah, 2004 and explores relationships and lives of soldiers during an investigation of the suspicious deaths of three soldiers supposedly killed by friendly fire.

SETTING: A bare stage except for the FEMALE SOLDIER.

SCENE: The FEMALE SOLDIER addresses the audience while on Sentry duty.

FEMALE SOLDIER

I was stationed in Kuwait, Camp Udairi, about 15 kilometers from the Iraqi border, awaiting deployment. It felt safe there. So, when I woke up in the middle of the night and needed to pee, I didn't think twice about walking to the latrine. I was just stepping in when I heard a noise. I started to turn to see what had made the sound, when something slammed into my head. I dropped, stunned, and then was hit again, this blow knocking me out cold.

I came to a little later with some guy on top of me, raping me. He was heavy and had me pinned. My hands were tied. He had stuffed my underwear in my mouth. As he fucked me, he growled if I resisted he'd cut my throat. I tried to talk through my gag when he hit me with the handle of the knife knocking me unconscious again.

When I regained consciousness, my hands were untied, my underwear thrown alongside me. I hurried back to the barracks. I was taken to an aid station. A rape examination was performed. They bandaged the cut on my head. I filled out a report. They assured me they'd get the guy. I was given a weeks' leave to recover from the attack, and that was that.

Nobody followed up. Whenever I'd ask about it they told me everything would be okay and to concentrate on getting well. My unit shipped outside Fallujah the next day. Later, one of my girlfriends back at Udairi wrote to tell me that a couple of male soldiers told her they heard it was my fault. They told her I had sneaked out to meet a guy and then, when I tried to change my mind, he raped me.

They felt sorry for the guy. Called me a P.T. and said I deserved it. I shut up after that. But I haven't forgotten. I didn't see the guy. I don't know what he looks like. Every time some male says hello to me I think it could be him, mocking me, waiting to do it again. And the goddamn headaches won't go away. Christ, I'm trapped in Fallujah. Even now, after the main push, there's fighting. I keep praying a sniper will get me. Please. I just want this nightmare to end.

MURDERED INNOCENCE

From the full-length drama, *Children of Shame*
By W. Colin McKay

BACKGROUND: During the Bosnia-Serbia conflict, MOLLY HINSON is working as a contract investigator for the U.N. War Crimes Tribunal. She's reluctantly agreed to interview a Christian missionary who works in the middle of Bosnia who has evidence for the Tribunal. The major problem is that the missionary in question is a Brigadier in the world famous Christian Missionary Army and, while Molly despises missionaries in general, she hates the Christian Missionary Army. SETTING: Outside of the prayer room in the mission. SCENE: The missionaries have revealed they know MOLLY had been raped and made pregnant as a teen and placed in a Christian Missionary Home. She lost the baby and turned against God. They want to know why.

MOLLY

Alright! I'll tell you. I hated it! So what? For three months I felt that damned thing inside me. I couldn't stand it. I couldn't go to school. I couldn't leave the Christian Missionary Army home where my folks had placed me. I hated those boys for what they had done to me. I hated my parents and those goddamn missionaries at the home. And, most of all, I hated my baby. Everyday damn day I went to chapel and prayed to God for forgiveness for whatever I had done to make Him let those boys rape me. I prayed to Him to let me have the baby, so I could take it around town, show everyone what had happened to me. I'd name the fathers. Point them out. Make the whole town hate them as much as I did.

When I ran away from the home, before they caught me, I confronted one of the boys who had raped me and told him what I planned for his baby. He begged me to get rid of it. I laughed at him. I wanted to ruin his life. Then. . . I miscarried.

I couldn't believe it. God let me be raped, let them have me one after another, and then took away my instrument of revenge. I cried for days, hating God. The sonofabitch erased the one thing that could've made my life. . . acceptable.

Then, later, I realized what had really happened. When I saw other babies, other mothers, saw how much they loved them, how much they were loved in return, I wanted to love my baby. I wanted my baby...to love. . . not hate.

    (beat)

At that moment, I realized God hadn't taken away my revenge. He had done something much worse. He had taken away the one chance I had had to make something ugly into something beautiful. He had murdered innocence and hope. He had killed love. The goddamn bastard but kept the evil alive… Fuck God.

MINUTES—MORE PLEASE

From the one-act comedy, *Time After Time*
By W. Colin McKay

BACKGROUND: This play is a farcical, non-linear exploration of relationships that serve as stumbling blocks to personal goals.
SETTING: A bare stage, with actors entering and exiting from non-specific areas, addressing the audience in the middle of a scene, and moving casually from light to dark.
SCENE: Clearly distraught, GLORIA addresses the audience.

GLORIA

I guess the only way to say it clearly would be to say again what I said earlier while saying, as clearly as possible, the only thing that could be said at the time. I'm an addict. I'm not smart. I know that. But I'm smart enough to know when I'm addicted to something. Yeah, I'm an addict.

(Takes a breath, begins)

Last night was when I realized all these years I'd been addicted and didn't know. Last night. After we had sex. It was then. Right then. That very moment. In an instant, I recognized my addiction. Oh, God forgive me, for taking so long to see. I'm addicted to ------- minutes!

(to tune of Mickey Mouse song)

M-I-N-U-T-E! Minutes are for me!

> (falls to knees)

MINUTES! Oh, God, minutes, minutes sprawled all over the floor. I see them.

> (starts "scraping up" minutes)

Do you see them? I do. I do. But they slip through my fingers. can't catch them. Oh, God. Oh, God. I used to have so many.

> (staggers up, clutching minutes in arms)

When I was a kid I had plenty. They surrounded me like a tomb. I couldn't breathe. They were a burden. Too heavy. I threw them away.

> (throws them at audience)

Gave them away to stupid people just to get rid of them. Stupid, stupid people like James Martinez, at the movies. We'd make out. He'd open my blouse and feel me up. I let him. I didn't like him a whole lot. But he had big hands. What the hell, right? I had minutes to spare. Might as well spend them letting him feel me up – I mean, I was young. I still had minutes to waste.

Sure, I could see a trail of minutes behind me, but there were waves of them ahead of me. Then one day everything was just perfect. Right number of minutes behind me. Right number ahead of me. By then I was married. . . to a musician. His idea of minutes was to get stoned and look the other way as the minutes crumbled. I went along. We'd be dancing, moving around the swirling minutes believing they were dancing with us. We believed that. Hell, they weren't dancing, they were making a mass get-away. Never entered our minds anything was the matter. Never entered our minds they were speeding us up to become matter.

(sucks in huge breath of air, finally exhales)

Holding my breath doesn't stop time. Even if I pass out. You know, when I was young, I used to live by the motto, "Live fast. Die young. Leave a good looking corpse." It's too late now. I've slowed down. I'm no longer young. . . Hell, I'd be a corpse with saggy boobs.

FROM 'GHANISTAN

From the full-length drama, *Zone of Separation*
By W. Colin McKay

BACKGROUND: TONI HARRIS is a female Army veteran who served four top-secret deployments in Afghanistan only to be sent home mentally exhausted, battling for her sanity. She tries to regain stability by being a stand-up comic.

SETTING: Bare stage except for microphone for comics.

SCENE: TONI performs one of her comic routines

TONI

Good evening. My name's Toni Harris, or, as the comics backstage call me, The-Beautiful-Lesbian-Back-From-'ghanistan. Hey, gotta tell ya! They'd never admit it, but they're jealous I'm gay. I mean, jealous! Every night I get to go home, tickle some pussy, grab a handful of boobs, and drink good wine. Even if I'm alone. Those dumb bastards go home, pick their noses, grab their cock, and drink cheap beer. Looooossssssers!

(sings out)

The horny Isis fighter in Troy,

Captured a lezzie but thought her a boy.

He planned to play in his room.

And there met his doom.

The "boy" brought her knife as a toy.

> (change of tone)

Hey, I've got a new car. A corvette! Convertible! It is sleek! It is slick. It is faster than a bad thought. Plan to paint it red. Red. Oh, yeah! Cherry red! Oooohhhh!

> (Seductive, rubs thighs, stops, steps to audience
>
> Speaks low, secretively)

Minor problem. Until I paint it, change plates. Don't let the owner know I've got it.

> (moans again)

A fancy forged plate.

> (breathing hard)

Just thinking about that red paint makes me a quivering mound of love pudding. Makes my girlfriend jealous I won't let her drive. Hell, if she drives, who'll push. On what I make here, I can't afford gas.

> (stupid-curtsies to left and right)

That's it, folks. Toni Harris. Fixed coordinates. Every Thursday. Same time. Same place. Come and get it.

CHAPTER 2

MONOLOGUES FOR MEN

W. Colin McKay

A SPECIFIC CAUSE

From the serio-comic full-length play, *Liberty Injustice*
By W. Colin McKay

NOTE: *THIS play is an attack on the politics behind the War in Iraq, which, seventeen years later is still being fought. The story which drives "Liberty Injustice" deals with the United States government's attempt to silence an American lawyer, Martha Bentley, defending an Iranian sheik who the government labels a terrorist. Throughout the play the STAGE MANAGER addresses the audience, comments on action onstage, jumps into a scene whether he is initially part of it, or not, or, in turn, becomes the audience.*

SETTING: Martha Bentley's living room.
SCENE: The STAGE MANAGER, addresses the audience after Martha Bentley agrees to defend the Iranian sheik over the warnings of her husband.

STAGE MANAGER

So you think this lady is cognizant of the specific classification of people she's up against? They have no respect for the law. They do anything, say anything, lie or cheat to get what they want. And if it's currently out of reach, they plan ahead. What they do today is in preparation for years from now. No hurry. They smile at the people, tell them to close their eyes and don't peek while they change, modify, adapt, or eliminate, a law with one hand and, with the other, when no one is looking, train an attack dog.

In May 2002, for instance, the Attorney General announced the elimination of a twenty-six-year-old regulation that had prevented the FBI from monitoring "open to the public" events held by domestic religious, political, and civic organizations unless it had specific cause for doing so. For twenty-six years it had worked nicely. But, because there was no brouhaha surrounding it, nobody minded much when it was changed. It seemed clerical. Not surgical.

Two years later, on February 3, 2004, the FBI Joint Terrorism Task Force, served subpoenas on Drake University. And, you ask, in what hideous evil had Drake University engaged? Indeed, what terrible dastardly deed did Drake do? Well. . . Drake University, that seething, leftist hotbed of controversy, had sponsored a conference in November 2003 that was. . . an anti-war conference. Oh no! How could that be? The conference had been about bringing the Iowa National Guard back from Iraq. Then, if that wasn't evil enough, following the conference there had been. . . a peaceful demonstration at the National Guard Training Center. Lo and be-screwed, the FBI had been monitoring. It was legal. Remember that law eliminated two years before?

The FBI subpoenaed, *demanding* in a rather *demanding* all records recorded by Drake University campus security officers, including their observations of the conference whether directly observable observations or not, including any records recorded relating to the people in charge, or to any of the attendees. In addition, the subpoenas sought information about the local chapter of. . . the oft-considered left-wing by the certainly honorable right-wing-wrapped-in-the-flag-of-the-United-States--carrying a copy of the U.S. constitution right up…well, no need being graphic. . . let's just say they carried it where the sun don't shine--and I'm not talkin' moonshine--and they carried it but never read it. Yessireeee, they gathered their forces and stood before the National Lawyers Guild and announced, that 'Because of, in deference to, referring about, according to stats it has been determined that, from, and, so on, and so on, and therefore, and whatnot, it is our judgment that the National Lawyers Guild from this day forth be known as. . . The *Evil* National Lawyers Guild.

And what had they done to garner such a harsh punishment? They had helped organize the conference. Fortunately, the lawyers won the battle over the right to privacy and the subpoenas were withdrawn. And the FBI were furious. And the bad guys hunkered down in their caves to watch for another chance to screw someone they hate. But as for Drake. . . Whew! Close! Free!

For the moment. Just for now. Just until. . . next time.

(pause)

In 1976, Supreme Court Justice William Douglas wrote: "As night-fall

43

does not come at once, neither does oppression. In both instances, there is a twilight when everything remains seemingly unchanged. And it is in such twilight that we all must be most aware of change in the air, however slight, lest we become unwitting victims of the darkness." It's strange, but whether you like it or not, you are in a change. It is changing all about you. The fabric we stand on is waving, creating deep folds that are awkward to manage. And there's a glow. See it? Over there.

        (points)

And there.

        (points another direction)

And ...

        (points to flag that is lowered from above)

And there ...

        (The flag slowly lifts. As it does, the STAGE
        MANAGER waves goodbye)

Don't forget me. We have forgotten you. Bye. Bye.

        (the stage goes dark)

PAY YOU BACK, PROMISE

From the full-length dark comedy, *Where Nobody Belongs*
By W. Colin McKay

BACKGROUND: RED is an alcoholic, who has a million reasons why people should loan him money. None of the reasons are true. He takes whatever money he gets and spends it on booze. His daughter has come into money but keeps it from Red.

SETTING: Street corner around from Red's favorite bar.

SCENE: Red is asking a drinking buddy for money "to go back home to Tucson."

RED

I'm asking my good friend, my best friend, who's like a brother, like my very own brother, for just enough money to go back home to Tucson. If I can get out of this lousy city I'll be a new man. I know it. Christ, when I was in Tucson, I was happy. Maybe I could be happy again. I want to get married, but I can't meet any women who'll even talk to me let alone marry me. These Los Angeles women are all alike. I tell them I love them. I open my heart to them. But as soon as I ask them for a little money for a pint of booze so we can celebrate our engagement, they cry out as if I shoved a burr up their butt, and accuse me of loving them only for their money. That's not true. I drink so I can be better company for them. I don't have to drink. I can stop whenever I want. I know they like champagne and all I'm doing is getting them what they like. I don't get it. It makes me sad they don't trust me. They don't understand the only reason I drink is because I'm unhappy. Okay, okay, I can tell from your look you're getting ready to tell me I was drinking in Tucson. That was different. I was drinking then because I was happy. That's an entirely different type of drinking. Come on, just loan me the money so I can do that kind of happy drinking again. Look upon it as a good deed. You want me to be happy, right?

(abrupt change to threatening)

Just loan me the goddamn money, you cheap bastard! You've got it! Don't try and tell me about your sister. You're not giving her a dime. You greedy fuck. I bet you'd screw your sister if she said she'd give you money. Or booze. You cheap bastard! Share it! Give me what I asked or . . .

(he hesitates, aware of what he had said, changes tone)

Hey, man, none of that's true. I don't know why I said it. You're a good guy. Everyone knows that. It was booze talking. I had a quick shot before coming over. Kick up my nerves. I'm sorry, man.

(his whine begins to dissipate)

I'm sorry. Honest. I didn't meant it. I. . .

(voice trails off, after a moment he looks up, hopefully)

I'll pay you back this time. I promise.

HIM OR ME

From the full-length drama, *Fallujah*

By W. Colin McKay

BACKGROUND: The play takes place after the Battle for Fallujah, 2004

SETTING: Empty battlefield after engagement

SCENE: The RAPPER serves as narrator, commenting on action within the play and on events occurring within the larger battle.

RAPPER

(speaks)

It's been flash bang for a week! Fallujah is nothing but bricks, strewn mortar and dead bodies, and enemy, lots of them, waiting to get you alone in a street, waiting to cut your head off, stomp you, hate you, waiting for you to come in so they can take you apart piece by piece.

(rap)

Your hands are hot, heart weak, arms scared,

Sweaty wrists, in your eyes, dark haired,

You're peeing warm, but looking cool

so damn ready to take the fool

In the streets they come for you, wanting you

Daring you, killing you,

drive you out, Day in, day out,

Drive'em south, corner'em out,

all day, all day

All the man can say

is kill'em now, kill the fuckers!

In the doorways, in the windows, behind the bars

Death waits, death calls, in halls, in cars.

Hides his face, confuses you,

is a kid,

is a girl

Open fire!

Don't! Wait!

Don't wait, too late

Fallujah! Fallujah! Can't go back, not this time

Not this time, last time, wrong time,

guys hanging, bodies black, tear'em down

Fallujah! Fallujah!

Don't look the guy you've shot

Don't see the guy you shot.

His kids!

Not your kids.

Him or me. Him or me.

Rat-tat, rat-tat, where's that? Rattatat reality

Fallujah, you motherfuckers.

Fallujah, assholes!

Who am I! We are! You aren't! We are! –

Word for you!

(mimics rapid fire, mimics rapidly firing rifle)

Dead! Dead! Dead! -- Dead! Dead! Dead -- Dead! Dead! Dead! -- Dead!

Dead! Dead! -- Dead! Dead! Dead! -- Dead! Dead! Dead!

DEAD!

I MISS HIM!

From the full-length drama, *Gentleman's War*

By W. Colin McKay

NOTE: The play <u>Gentleman's War</u> *is set in South Africa, 1900, during the South African War (Boer War). The South African War pitted the British Army against the Dutch Boers in a battle for geo-political supremacy of South Africa. It also served as the catalyst for the decades-long rule of apartheid. COLONEL CLARK-HOWELLL is one of the main characters and is fashioned somewhat after Colonel Baden-Powell of Boy Scouts fame. While the story is fictional, it is loosely based on Colonel Baden-Powell's experience as a commander during the actual Boer blockade of Mafeking, South Africa.*

BACKGROUND: The British have occupied a town by the name of Graysmith, but in so doing find themselves surrounded by Boers. The commanding officer is a delicate Colonel who sings and dances for the entertainment his troops and the town he governs. He praises his own ability as a scout and has a "special" relationship with one of his boys training to also be a scout. JEDEDIAH CARSON, an American reporter for a major San Francisco newspaper sent to observe the few Americans fighting for the Boers, is apprehended by British forces. The British suspect that he may be a spy for the Boers. Jed is detained in Graysmith, the town occupied by the British. However, the town is surrounded by Boers. The inhabitants of the occupied town are allowed to go about their daily business. One of the inhabitants is the widow, KATIE McKINNON, an East Indian who had been married to a British officer killed early in the conflict. She now runs a boarding house in Graysmith. During the period of his confinement, JEDIDIAH is housed at KATIE McKINNON's boarding house. They are drawn to each other.

SETTING: KATIE's house

SCENE: KATIE and JED have had sex for the first time.

CLARK-HOWELL

Oh, my God, what will I do without the boy? ~~Nobody but he understood~~. Now what am I going to do?

(building to a wild pitch)

I'd been given secret orders! Only Boy Wilson and I knew. ~~Nobody else. Only us.~~ You see, the British knew that war would break out soon. ~~You'll write this down! They were afraid of the Boers moving in on too many fronts~~. We weren't ready for this war. All we had ever fought were natives. ~~. . .for years and years and years. We hadn't~~ fought white men. They knew that the Boers would want Graysmith… but only as a symbol . . . a quick victory to brag about. It has no strategic importance. But the British Army didn't want to give them any victory. I was sent here and told to hold out for as long as I could and then retreat, give the Army time to get down here in force. Graysmith was not important. I was not important. Hold, then retreat. The newspaper headline would read, "Clark-Howell retreats!" I was nothing more than a holding action.

Well, I did more than hold. I stopped the Boers. I wouldn't give up. And the Siege of Graysmith began. By the end of the first month of the Siege, the British army was organized, the war was underway, and they thought Graysmith was no longer needed, but I held on. I made the town believe we were important. Especially the stupid journalists trapped here. They began writing of the hardships, the bravery. The leadership.

All of which I gave them. They were too lazy to go out and look for themselves. They relied on me to give them the news. They took what I said as true and wrote it down.

(laughs and dances about)

After awhile we began getting reports back that the English papers were full of Graysmith. I had become important. I am important. Then, I was ordered to abandon Graysmith. The Generals were jealous of my growing fame. They wanted me to fail. I couldn't do that. I cabled back if they ordered me to abandon Graysmith I would tell everyone what they had done, that they had given me orders to surrender to the Boers, ~~they had ordered~~ Graysmith to be lost. I asked ~~them if they wanted that in the papers?~~

You see, Mr. Carson, by then the Boers were winning battles. The British Army was being humiliated. They needed ~~to have~~ a victory. ~~Needed it.~~ And, suddenly, unimportant, ~~non-strategic,~~ Graysmith, was their one ~~overwhelming~~ victory. If the generals took that away, ~~if they had dared,~~ there would've been the devil to pay. ~~Suddenly, there were Army cables telling me to keep up the good work.~~ Newspapers at home heralded, "Graysmith: The greatest military battle since Nelson at Trafalgar."

All the while I knew Graysmith was safe! ~~The town, the people, were in no danger!~~

(giggling in delight at he speaks)

Mr. Carson, while it was true that we were surrounded, and that the Boers wouldn't give up, that they didn't want to suffer a "loss" --- I also knew they didn't want to waste too many men ~~for a place of such little military worth.~~ You see, I had scouted the Boers. ~~I saw they had mostly gathered up and gone to fight for more strategic areas and had left behind just enough men to fire the cannon every now and then but not too often.~~ I saw they had left very little ammunition and shells.

I knew if we had charged them, we would've won. But I would've lost. So, I remained here. We were safe, but ~~I continued to create in everyone's mind the dangerous threat of the Boers. A menace.... that was not real.~~ I had out-tricked them all. ~~I told you I was tricky.~~

But then that murderous Bantu began killing my men. ~~It had to be a Bantu.~~ We couldn't catch him. ~~I tried!~~ Oh, God, I tried! ~~I couldn't catch him.~~ If I had… ~~Oh, God,~~ Boy Wilson would still be alive, ~~wouldn't he?~~ He'd still be here! ~~My poor young boy.~~ He was so ~~young, so gallant. His strong body.~~ So brave. ~~Oh, Boy Wilson.~~ He ~~was to be the~~ head scout. He ~~was to be my pride~~ and joy. He was ~~perfection. He would've been… Oh, God, he was so important to me. How can I live without him?~~ You must make him a god when you write about him. True. Brave. ~~He must've died heroically.~~ Struggling ~~to the end. Outnumbered. Fighting for his life. Not caught by surprise by some contemptible Bantu, not twisted and held powerless, his throat cut, and his dead body dumped into a burial pit with dogs. No! He must die gloriously!~~ His death must serve as an example to all scouts ~~who follow after him as~~ the model of dedication to duty, willingness to complete a task or die in the attempt. ~~Loyal to his office~~rs.

~~I will not let ungodly, vile black creatures take from me something so dear, so exquisite as the Boy Wilson.~~ Oh, God, I miss his sweet smile. His elegant voice. I wish it would've been me. . . ~~I miss him!~~

KID UNDERWATER

From the Reader's Theatre, *Hitman Blues*

By W. Colin McKay

BACKGROUND: A mob HITMAN stops for the night on his way to a "job".

SETTING: A cheap motel bar in the afternoon.

SCENE: The HITMAN is sitting at a bar, recalling a moment without an ending.

HITMAN

You know, my presence usually means a life is going to end. But, well, not always.

It happened about ten years ago. Motel somewhere. I'm not sure. It's either Tucson, Arizona or Bakersfield, California. Oh, well. Either place. Same thing. Armpit of the world. What happens to anyone, who cares? Anyway, I decide to splash around in the motel pool. But, as I approach it, I can hear a husband and wife arguing about the best way to teach their kid to swim. The argument's heated, but I figure it's all theoretical. I mean, they're screaming about their kid in the third person. He's not there, right? Wrong. I get closer and see him, very much in the first person, standing off to one side. He's about nine years old. Perspiration is coming off him like Niagara Falls and every time one of his parents mentions the pool, his whole body, from top to bottom, convulses in fear. He stands there, frozen in place, staring at the horrible swamp of doom without even a diving board.

Bam! Out of nowhere, his father, an ape of a guy, lunges for the kid, jerks him off his feet, and thrusts the poor kid through the air straight toward the death swamp. The panicked kid screams in terror as he flies to his fate. He grunts as he belly flops. Silently floats for a moment. Then, sinks. In the meantime, all hell breaks loose poolside. Mom yells, "What the hell have you done?" The father yells louder, "Try to make a man out of him."

Mom accuses the father of a being an insensitive brute. The father beats his chest and accuses the mother of making the kid a mama's boy. The mother calls him, "her angel." The father calls her "obsessive" and says the trouble with the kid is that she, "can't get her tit out of his mouth." Whammo! The only thing stopping them from coming to blows is a green plastic table and a chair sitting between them as a sort of no-man's land. I'm telling you that damn poolside argument is so exciting, nobody notices the kid's under water – down for the count.

Well, at that point, I consider going back to my room and staying out of the drama, what's one more dead kid? But, well, goddamn it, the kid's drowning. He's not dead yet, right? For some reason and even now, I don't know why, I dive in, yank him to the top and drag him poolside. He's sucking in air like a vacuum cleaner, but he's breathing.

I pat him on the back to let him know he's going to be okay. Well, anyway, the parental tsunami continues its surge around us, completely unaware of the kid and me. Father throws a pool chair. Mother heaves an ashtray. He shoves the table in the pool. She throws his cigarettes in after it.

That does it!

He chases her around the deck threatening to body-slam her in the shallow end. Amidst all this, I grab a towel lying on someone's lounge chair, wrap the kid as best I can, and take him inside to the motel bar.

I order a Gin and Tonic for me and cover him for a Cuba Libre. It's booze, but it's got coke. I figure the kid needs it. By then, everyone knows about the family brawl going on at the pool. The bartender serves us, no charge. The kid turns to me and says, "Thank you. Saving me was a very nice thing to do. I hope it didn't inconvenience you." He's nine fucking years old and worrying about "inconveniencing" me. I tell him I'm not inconvenienced. He then looks at me with this long, apologetic face and says, "It was quite unnecessary. After the first few moments, I found the thought of dying acceptable, even desirable."

What do you say to that? I bought him another Cuba Libre, double, and went back to my room. The next morning, they tell me his family left early. Nobody can remember the kid being with them.

BURN THE STORE DOWN

From the comedy one-act play, *Burning Issue*
By W. Colin McKay

BACKGROUND: Ellen Wilson's book store has gone bankrupt.
SETTING: FRANKLIN HOLLY, well dressed, well spoken, enters the store just before Ellen is going home.
SCENE: FRANKLIN is trying to convince Ellen Wilson to burn down her bankrupt bookstore and collect the insurance money.

FRANKLIN

My mom died giving birth to me. That left Pop with his grocery store and me. When I was about ten years old a market about two blocks away, which had never done very well, burned down. It was very suspicious, but the insurance company paid off. The owner used the money from the insurance to rebuild a bigger store with lower prices, and started taking away our customers. Being quick-witted, Pop burned our store down.

He took the money from the insurance, opened another store several miles away, just like you want to do, by the way, and we did very well, better than we had ever done. My father told some our friends who had small businesses what he had done and helped them burn down their stores so they could open newer ones, and so forth and so forth. By the time he died two years ago, he had helped almost a hundred businesses. All for free. No strings. He helped because he believed in the red, white, and blue.

Pop wanted nothing else but to be a good American. Same with me. Big business drove you out. Big business crushes the little guy. Big business is not a good American. We support the little guy. How American can you get? Besides, don't worry about it. I've checked. . . . You've paid your premiums and--for what you paid--you deserve a good fire.

SISSY YANK

From the comedy screenplay, *Used Blood*
By W. Colin McKay

BACKGROUND: In this farcical screenplay, **BOORAH** is an over-the-top go-and-get-'em type. He's been purposely sent on a suicide mission by the government. The government hopes to both get rid of a heavily protected cartel drug lord and, at the same time, get rid of **BOORAH.** Unfortunately for the government, they only get rid of the drug cartel lord. **BOORAH** completes the suicide mission.

SETTING: Temporary camp before attacking the cartel in the morning

SCENE: Boorah telling of the horrific torture he endured when captured by enemy forces in Vietnam.

BOORAH

For a full twenty-four hours the torture continued. First, they tied me to a stake and then they surrounded me, chanting over and over, "Sissy, Yankee. Sissy, Yankee." They called me a sissy! The shame of it! They're calling me hurtful names. Trying to break me. But I resisted. Then they forced me to eat…yogurt. Fat old ladies eat yogurt.

(crying out in memory)

A fat, old ladies, yogurt. Christ, I'd have rather eaten a fat old lady.

(shudders)

After that, they made me dress like a girl. Have you ever worn panty hose? Dirty panty hose? Two sizes too small? Ohhhh, the humiliation. The memory is ghastly. Why couldn't they have just cut my balls off and let me bleed to death like a man? Later, when I told the brass about the torture, about what I had had to endure, they laughed. Out loud. They laughed! At me! I'll never forget. I will never forgive them.

(almost a whisper)

They will pay!

M-16 GLADIATORS

From the full-length drama, *Fallujah*

By W. Colin McKay

BACKGROUND: The play takes place after the Battle for Fallujah, 2004.

SETTING: A chair and computer on a desk onstage.

SCENE: A CORPORAL, U.S. Army comes on, sits and begins typing, he talks as he does.

CORPORAL

Hey, Bro, hope you're reading your email. They've got all these computers set up for writing home. Hey, some guys have even set up their own blogs. Geez, I know it may seem kinda funny, I love it here. They stuck me in supplies. It's great here. Burger King. Pizza Hut. Air conditioned barracks. Got my X-box going all the time. I'm king of Halo 2. Movies. All the DVD's you want. All the cowboy movies you could ask for. Jesus, Bro, and on top of everything we get great food. Catered. Man, it's the life here. Like a big, all paid for, vacation.

Other day we played Gladiator. We recreated Roman gladiator fights. We covered our helmets with tinfoil and that type of shit, made bats into spiked weapons, made maces out of baseballs, spiked both the bats and maces with M-16 rounds, and went to it. Man, it was something. We took some horses from some of the local Hajis, hitched them to wagons, and had chariot races and battles. We do that kind of thing all the time. Bro, sure, some guys die over here, but shit, more of the enemy die than us. Last I heard we had over a 10-1 kill ratio. Sometimes, better. They'll run out of insurgents at that rate. I hope not. Don't want it to end too soon.

Hey, bro, you want women? There's women everywhere. All branches! I can't do as much as I want right now, because there's something wrong with my balls or something. The doc said he'd figure it out. Naw, it's not what you think, bro. It's something else. Not catchable. Bro, I don't know how to tell you, but this is the place. The way we keep building new bases I figure we're planning on staying here forever. If so, I'm a lifer. This is too good!

ATTACKED BY SHADOWS

From the full-length drama, *Shadow War*

By W. Colin McKay

NOTE: Shadow War *is based on a true story.*

BACKGROUND: GENERAL FREDRICK FUNSTON was in charge of the American forces during the War in the Philippines, circa 1901. America promised the Philippines political freedom if they helped the United States drive Spain out of the islands. However, after defeating Spain, the United States reneged on its promise and retained control of the Philippines and put in its own government. There was an immediate insurrection, which the United States set about to end. Because they didn't have the same resources as the military from America, the Filipino freedom-fighters engaged in guerilla warfare in a manner similar to what the United States faced decades later in Vietnam, and now faces in the Middle East.

SETTING: GENERAL FUNSTON is alone writing on a desk.

SCENE: GENERAL FUNSTON explains to his wife the difficulty of fighting against guerilla warfare, occasionally stopping and looking for word.

FUNSTON

It's ghastly over here. Terrible. This isn't a war. Not in the real sense of the word. In a real war, there are enemies, actual enemies you can see, who stand up and fight. Here, there are only shadows. We'll be on patrol, moving through the jungle. It's hot. We're all sweating. Our steps are slow, careful. We're listening for the slightest sound. The forward men search the jungle for movement, trying to ferret out the most negligible of signs of enemy presence. But all they, or we, can see are tall, leafy trees covered with heavy foliage slowly swaying, casting shadows upon shadows.

It's quiet. Serene even. Maybe I'll see a flower I've never seen before, its beauty declaring the magnificence of God's love. I'll pause, break out a sketch pad. Bang! The jungle fills with gunfire. Bullets zinging past, smashing into mules and men. Men's screams match the piercing braying of wounded mules, both shrieking in denial as they die. There's no time to return fire. I fling myself on the ground, pull out my revolver. Suddenly it stops, quick as it began. Flash. Like that. Stops. I leap to my feet, desperately run to the edge of the skirmish, try to see who fired on us, who killed us.

Nothing. Nothing but quiet shadows moving with the hot breeze. Proving to the jungle we're not afraid, even though we're lying, we fire indiscriminately into the trees. We hit nothing, only air and blood-red steam. We cease shooting. Nothing more to prove. The jungle's calm again, underneath a clear, beautiful sky. Maybe the flower'll still be there. Only now, all around it, are dead soldiers. We'll pick them up, put them on the mules, and press forward as if nothing had happened.

(he stops writing and rips up letter, crying now)

So many men are dying. Killed by shadows.

WRONGFUL SUITS

From the screenplay, *Acceptable Risk*

By W. Colin McKay

NOTE: *This is a true story based on the worst single aircraft crash in the United States. It involved American Airlines and McDonnell Douglas.*

SETTING: A living room of a modest house.

SCENE: STERNS is a lawyer representing a spouse of one of the deceased passengers who is suing for damages. He is explaining to her the machinations of the legal system.

STERNS

Now the court battles really begin. Let me prepare you for what is about to occur. All sides. It'll begin with the arguments about where to hold the trial. Then, about whether the families of the dead can sue in their home states. Is that confusing? Easy. Some states allow for more damages. The more they can get, the harder they'll fight to move jurisdiction. Then they'll fight over whether or not it'd be best to sue McDonnell Douglas in St. Louis, where their main headquarters are located, or in Long Beach where the design headquarters are. The same for American. Where should the trials be held? New York? Chicago?

Maybe they'll fight over what type of death occurred. Did the passenger die from fright before the crash? Because, if he did, the crash didn't kill him. His heart did. Sure, the impending crash frightened him, but what if there hadn't been a crash? What if the plane survived losing the engine, and there'd been no crash? The guy would still be dead from a heart attack. Whose fault is that?

Maybe they'll even go so far as to try to decide in which state for which specific sub-sub-headquarter should individual suits take place? And then, what kind of suits? Was it caused by negligence? If so, by who? Maybe it's wrongful death? Maybe psychological abuse because of the terror felt by the passengers knowing they were going to crash? Mental anguish for the survivors? It'll go on and on. Their main weapon will be delay. And then more delay followed by more delay. The idea will be to wear... no ... to beat you down. To have you screaming "no more." To have you settle for less just to get the damn thing over with. When you finally get to that point, when you can't stand it anymore, when you're so exhausted you can't think straight, remember. Remember, I've been here before. Many times. And, you have my word, I'll get you through it. I will get you through it. I promise.

PISSING IN A TWISTER

From the full-length drama, *Nagasaki Dust*

By W. Colin McKay

BACKGROUND: RANDOLPH, a young military lawyer, has agreed to defend, John Okui, a Japanese-American in his early twenties charged with treason but who maintains his innocence. The United States Army wants the trial to "look fair" but is demanding that Randolph lose the case.

SETTING: Randolph alone onstage.

SCENE: Randolph addresses the audience and describes Military Justice, circa 1946.

RANDOLPH

My Pop once equated my being an Army defense lawyer to me standing in the middle of a twister and pissing in the wind. Of course, he said that to start an argument. God, he loved to argue. But before I had a chance to respond, he went on to say that comparing military justice to real justice was like comparing military music to real music. You see, he was offering me my choice of metaphors to defend or attack. He was not a rigid man. If I had passed on either one of those, I'm sure he would've had three or four others. I mean, Pop would've been disappointed if I hadn't chosen one. Like I said, he loved a good argument.

As military music was slightly less theoretical than standing in the middle of a twister, I chose the music metaphor. And so, we spent most of that night arguing about Beethoven. . . John Phillip Sousa. . . Oliver Wendell Holmes. . . and, finally, somehow, trying to decide if the *Stars and Stripes Forever*, did indeed, present a Clear and Present Danger to the listener.

It was a hell of night. But I remember, during the entire argument, being intrigued with the picture of me standing in the middle of a twister and pissing. . . and trying to decide if I would get wet, or if the water would just circle around me spattering everything else while I stayed dry. It was one of those questions, which I thought would always remain theoretical. Christ, who would've guessed?

      (beat)

You know what I liked best about the law? I believed. . . I believed to my core. . . that, after careful analysis, almost every argument would finally break down to an inevitable conclusion. I may not have liked it. I may have ignored it. Hell, I may even have denied it. But. . . it'd be there. I loved that concept: if you worked at something long enough and hard enough, the truth would spring forth.

The key was to make sure the analysis had been complete and thorough. You see, there are three main ingredients to any argument.

      (holds up one finger)

The data.

(holds up second finger)

The warrant. . . which links the data to that final, inescapable...

(holds up third finger)

Conclusion. Got it?

Okay, just in case. For example. Data--the airplane is on fire and is falling out of the sky. Warrant--airplanes which are on fire, and falling out of the sky, crash. Everybody onboard dies. Conclusion--get the hell out of the plane, dummy. See? Nothing to it. Except. . . except if you've been performing your analysis while urinating in the middle of a twister.

Data--the airplane is on fire and is falling out of the sky. Warrant--airplanes on fire and falling out of the sky crash, usually killing everyone onboard.

But. . . you can't get out of the plane because the Army has ordered you to stay in it until it crashes. So, if you follow orders, you'll die. On the other hand, if you bail out, you'll get court-martialed and shot. You die either way. Conclusion? You pee in the middle of a twister, everyone gets wet.

MACHINATIONS

From the serio-comic full-length play, *Hegal Got it Right*
By W. Colin McKay

NOTE: *This play is an agit-prop attack on the politics behind the War in Iraq. Utilizing an absurdist approach which features topical politicians and current sentiments, a play within a play, and audience participation. "Liberty Injustice" deals with the United States government's attempt to silence an American lawyer, Martha Bentley, defending an Iranian sheik who the government labels a terrorist. Throughout the play, the GREETER addresses the audience, comments on action onstage, jumps into a scene whether he is initially part of it, or not, or in turn, becomes the audience.*

SETTING: Bare stage with only spotlight following GREETER.
SCENE: THE GREETER addresses the audience. The GREETER, now wearing a jester's hat and an unbuttoned tunic, skips onto the stage.

GREETER

I can hear all the good patriots now offering thanks to God for Immigration enforcement. You hear them, too? Boy, do those guys feel safer now that we've got ICE rounding up illegal aliens. No matter how legal-like these illegal people have been living here or for how long. One year. Two. Thirty. It doesn't matter. They can all disappear without a word. So far, we're lucky we're not rounding up and shipping out, those who are genuinely legal like they did in the last century.

Hey, buckaroos, is everybody here aware that the word "citizen" doesn't appear in the Patriot Act when discussing penalties? Instead, we find the word "person." You know those rights granted citizens under the constitution? The right to, "due process under law"? Gone. Not just for foreigners but for us. United States citizens, uh persons. Oh, there's also "Domestic Terrorism." New word. No real definition. Defined by operation. That's anything you and I do which Donnie Trump and/or Stevie Miller, who wears the mask of former Army-guy Kelly and who really runs la Casa Blanca, could constitute as aiding terrorists.

You know, things like criticizing the government. Like writing this play. Being in it. Producing it. Even. . . watching it. Uh, being Muslim. You see, there is no definition of domestic terrorism beyond a general statement just as, there is no definition of enemy combatant beyond a general description. Now that one is up to Trump or Putin or whoever is making decisions in the White House. No one other than the President of the United States can declare someone an "enemy combatant." This all falls under *Authorization for Use of Military Force or AUMF.* Awyoumuf. I call it that.

As of 2013, Awyoumuf had been invoked more than 30 times to authorize troop deployments and other military measures, including detentions at Guantanamo Bay and military trials for terrorism suspects.

Summary, if Trumtin thinks you could be an enemy combatant: that's all that's needed for you to magically disappear from the streets. Representative Barbara Lee, a Democrat from California, co-authored a bipartisan bill stripping away many of those Trumtin powers, but Paul Ryan and his Blue Ass, uh, cow, uh, ox, arbitrarily stripped those strippings away, leaving the stripping stripped with no public vote or debate. I hope everyone notices the machinations coming in under the radar.

This all means, Tutin and Prump can authorize the detainment of citizens. . . uh, persons. . . for investigative purposes and conduct surveillance, even when there is no basis for suspecting terrorist activity. You ever heard of the "sneak and peek" warrant? Not to be confused with the Fourth Amendment's protection against unreasonable search and seizure. Well, this new and improved PATRIOT warrant permits agents to search homes and confiscate property without first notifying the owner. I'd say it's been used hundreds of times, but that'd be wrong. Try thousands of times.

That'd be right! Wow! Fun, huh?

Can't you just wait to see what Trump and Putin and Trumpet Enterprises can cook up in four years? Yippee! With a hey, vladdy, hey, donny, cry cuckoo! Cuckoo! CUCKOO!

TAG IT! BAG IT!

From the full-length drama, *Fallujah*
By W. Colin McKay

BACKGROUND: The play takes place after the Battle for Fallujah, 2004. The RAPPER serves as narrator, commenting on action of the play and events occurring within the larger battle.

SETTING: Newly fought battlefield, dead bodies scattered among remnants of battle.

SCENE: The RAPPER enters through smoke and haze of battle scene.

RAPPER
(speaking, not rap, but still rhythmic)
It's a large, makeshift building on the outskirts of Fallujah.
(points offstage)
We called it the Potato Factory. They said that's what it was before. Now, it's where dead bodies go after cleanup. When Fallujah calms down, in-between strikes, some of us receive orders to recover bodies and body parts and other dead shit, everyone calls us the Potato Pickers. Pretty funny, huh? Hell, we have more Mr. Potato Head jokes than dead terrorists! I mean, that's the kind of thing we look for, right? Arms. Legs. Heads.

(Rapping – slow, soft)

It's almost over you tell yourself.

Others die.

Brothers die.

Not me!

Turn back real-i-ty.

I live. Hide away.

No good! No good! Not okay.

Thought I'd got away.

The man from hell points at me!

Po-ta-to Fact-o-ry!

No, dude, not me.

No more! No more!

You hear 'em breathe, laugh, snicker.

They no potato picker.

(Faster, louder)

Body parts, on the ground, the ground,

Legs, arms, eyes, bloody mound.

Move quick. Move fast.

Our guys, their guys, move your ass!

Intestines, veins, hearts!

Body parts.

Did I do this one?

Did I do that one?

Kids, women, men, soldiers, ours, theirs,

Women dead, kids in shreds, puking, peeing.

Moving through the rat rubble.

Tag this!

Bag that!

Shovel it all. Shovel the shit!

Shovel!

Christ!

WE'RE IN HELL!

        (Speaking, stops rap)

I'm, standing here, standing in someone else's blood, someone else's crap, trying to simply figure out where I am. Then they come!

        (Points)

Jesus! Get'em! Get'em! Motherfucker! Get the dogs! Starving! Fighting. for the dead! Dogs! Packs! Goddamn it, shoot the dogs!

        (Raps again)

Starving! Snarling!

Tearing, carrying pieces of dead,

Jaws bloody, fur matted, slick with red.

Teeth bared, shoot'em, kill'em, I want'em dead!

Too many. Everywhere! Shoot, shoot, you assholes!

Forget your dog at home! Your dog's dead! Don't cry.

Christ! Don't cry! Not now! Don't cry!

NOT OVER DOGS!

        (Begins crying while still rapping)

Fucking dust, fucking flies, all over me.

Smell the stink.

Stink of shit, stink of dead, look, see.

Oh, fucking goddamn shit!

No more!

No more!

No more!

POTATO FACT-O-RY!

PROMISED

From the full-length drama, *Gentleman's War*

By W. Colin McKay

NOTE*: The play* <u>Gentleman's War</u> *is set in South Africa, 1900, during the South African War (Boer War). The South African War pitted the British Army against the Dutch Boers in a battle for geo-political supremacy of South Africa. It also served as the catalyst for the decades-long rule of apartheid. COLONEL CLARK-HOWELLL is one of the main characters and is fashioned somewhat after Colonel Baden-Powell of Boy Scouts fame. While the story is fictional, it is loosely based on Colonel Baden-Powell's experience as a commander during the actual Boer blockade of Mafeking, South Africa.*

BACKGROUND: The British have occupied a town by the name of Graysmith, but in so doing find themselves surrounded by Boers. The commanding officer is a delicate colonel who sings and dances for the entertainment his troops and the town he governs. He praises his own ability as a scout and has a "special" relationship with one of his boys training to also be a scout. JEDEDIAH CARSON, an American reporter for a major San Francisco newspaper sent to observe the few Americans fighting for the Boers, is apprehended by British forces. The

British suspect that he may be a spy for the Boers. Jed is detained in Graysmith. The inhabitants of the occupied town are allowed to go about their daily business. One of the inhabitants is the widow KATIE McKINNON, an East Indian, who had been married to a British officer killed early in the conflict. She now runs a boarding house in Graysmith. During his period of detainment, JEDEDIAH is housed at Katie's boarding house.

SETTING: Katie's house.

SCENE: JEDEDIAH tells Katie about himself after she and Jed had sex the previous evening for the first time.

JED

Look, Katie, things moved pretty fast last night and, well, damn it, I'm not like other guys who go about lying to women just to get their way. I hate being lied to, so I make it a point never to do it to anyone else. I don't know what's happened with us. It's caught me just as much by surprise as you. I mean, when I first came here, I thought maybe you'd be lonely, looking for a good time. But you pretty well made it clear right off that that wasn't the case. So, I backed off or I thought I did, or I meant to. You're a good-looking woman, Katie. Smart. Gentle. I'm not used to being around women like that. Something happened to me. Something I wasn't ready for. What I told you the other night was true. I've never met anyone like you. Katie, I like you. I like you a lot. If you'll let me, I'll stick by you. I promise. My word is true. As God is my witness, I'll keep that promise. I will.

NOT MUCH MORE

From the serio-comic full-length play, *Hegel Got it Right*

By W. Colin McKay

BACKGROUND: This play is an agit-prop attack on the politics behind the chaos in the United States government. Utilizing an absurdist approach, which features topical politicians and current sentiments, a play within a play, and audience participation, deals with the United States government's attempt to silence the media and expose the workings of government agencies. Throughout the play the GREETER addresses the audience, jumps into a scene whether he is initially part of it, or not, or, in turn, becomes the audience.

SETTING: This is the GEETER's opening speech, house lights full. The audience has no idea the play has begun until he enters.

SCENE: The GREETER comes on stage, dressed flamboyantly, circles about, and begins speaking.

GREETER

Okay, everyone, quiet down. Quiet. You guys in the booth, leave the house lights on.

(turns to audience, grins)

Whether you like it or not, we've begun. 'Course that's the way life is, isn't it? Things begin, run, end, whether we like or not. Nothing we can do about it. That's all we do, come and go. Hope somebody knew we were here. Notices when we're gone. We're at life's mercy. Okay, okay, not quite. We can kill ourselves and put an end to life! But most of us are too chicken to do that. We leave it up to fate and spend most of our time pretending we won't die until Fate says so. I mean, who knows, we might live forever, if Fate is kind. . . I suppose. Also, in your case here at the theater, you could leave. No money back, though. And, you'd miss this. A play. Everything you see is play. . . a play. . . playful.

(House lights begin to dim)

Damn it, I said leave them on!

(House lights come back up)

It's too easy to rationalize in the dark.

(assumes whiny voice)

"Couldn't see it, pal. I would've done something, but it was so damn dark!"

(smiles knowingly at audience, sing-song voice)

Too easy to pick your nose in the dark. To touch the girl next to you. To fall asleep. To sneak a peek for a forbidden view up the dress behind. . . in the dark.

(normal voice).

Yep, dark's good. Light's bad. Nobody likes it when the light's on him or her. Okay, about now you're wondering who the hell I am, and what the hell is going on, and when in hell is the play going to start, and you're probably thinking to yourself what in the hell am I doing here when I can be home watching TV? Last first you're watching a play. I told you. And you're not going to see this on TV. Reverse order, the play's started, the play's going on, and I'm your guide.

It's set in the future. Like a minute from now. Well, maybe more. But not much more. Oh, you didn't ask what kind of play. Agit-prop! That's right. Agit-prop! Never heard of it? Agit-prop means we believe one thing and we say so. Like television pundits. You know, like Sean Hannity, Ann Coulter, Fox News...Rachel Maddow, Lawrence O'Donnell, MSNBC. Uh, like me.

>(assumes boisterous, passionate voice of pulpit preacher)

We believe! Good God Almighty, we believe!

>(assumes regular voice)

Of course, you know which of that group believe the truth and which believe lies. Anyhoo, agit-prop means we don't have to do a play. We don't have to do any of the normal things. We can drag one of you up here, cut your heart open, and build a symbolic tribute to the violent nature of peace over your dead body. Of course, we won't do that. You believe me, right? I mean, I wouldn't want any of you thinking we're going to do anything untoward to any audience member. No, we wouldn't do that. .... Would we?

HOLD IT – HOLD IT

From the readers theatre script, *Dogsbody*

By W. Colin McKay

BACKGROUND: **DEREK** is a psychic, who is paid great sums of money to find people whether they are alive or dead. If they are dead, he can tell how they died. At this moment, he is on vacation and has no interest in finding anyone. He spends a great deal of time in a bar, which both blocks his psychic ability and serves as a hiding place among others who wish to remain hidden for their own reasons.

SETTING: a bar

SCENE: DEREK is seated at a bar table. He sees someone enter the bar.

DEREK

(He turns to audience)

I spot him as an "irregularity" from his first step into the place. Can't miss him. A fish out of water. Well dressed, clean, sober. More than can be said about anyone else in here, including me. But, none of us are so drunk as to be unable to process what his presence means or threatens. In here, nobody knows anybody else. . . in here. But at this moment, at this precise moment, we momentarily bond, one with the other, watchful, taking stock, together. I can hear our cumulative breaths sucking air in, sighing out, sucking in (asking together, what's going down?), sighing out, (hearing together, more vehicles pulling up?), sucking in, (armed men, swarming the bar, who are they here for), hold it, hold it, (who?) sighing out, (eyes on me?) sucking in, hold it, hold it, (Me! I was afraid of that. They're here for me.), the collective sigh gives out, breathes easier, except for. . . me. I watch, amused, as the bond breaks and one by one, those, who seconds ago shared my breath, physically distance themselves from me, terrified I might forget the rules of order in here, call out to any of them. . . by name. My amusement remains quiet as they glide away. And, as they glide, they flash deferential smiles to the armed reinforcements (a crouching thanks for having been left alive) with only an occasional, cowering glance of curiosity or pity tossed my direction.

Instinctively, I start to reach to my immediate left for the black, sateen curtain covering my personal passage out. Wait. A soft rustling of pants legs from the void beyond the curtain. Okay. Relax. The ambush has been successful. Time for mental notes. General question number one: who? Quick assessment. Him. At the bar. The boss is the one standing at the bar, holding his drink at a slight angle so anyone, that is, anyone who cares about such things, could see the cut of the tumbler and recognize, if they were into recognizing such things, he's ordered an old fashioned. Stylish drink. Everything old is new again. He shifts his weight. Nice shoes. Suit too. Linen. Stylish cut. Everything about you is stylish, isn't it? Within moderation, of course. Sleek, but not too sleek. Restrained.

You know those who yell and beat their chests drown out their power, losing it in the very chaos they create. Absolute power is silent. You're moving. Turning your body toward me, presenting yourself for my appreciation. Trim, solid body. Square shoulders. Muscular hands. Long fingers. Face carved from bleached stone. Hard blue eyes. Arrogant eyes. A smug prig who's accustomed to your presence being enough to silence any who might want to speak up and, maybe, say the wrong words. Do that, and they're dead. Maybe literally. I wonder. How high is your personal body count?

Well, well. What do you know? You're stepping away from the bar. Finally. And in my direction. Want to be personal. General mental note number two: this guy saunters. Powerful. Dangerous. Each step he takes lets the air out of time.

General mental question: what are you doing here, buddy? I guess I'll have to wait until you start talking and figure it out then. Hold it. You just looked away for a moment, startled by a cough. One of your guys coughed. What's with that? One cough. You jumped. What's with the timidity? Hold it. Hold it. Yeah. That's it. Damn it, that's it. You're not the boss, hot shot. You're not the initiator of the action. You're here because someone said you *had* to come. That's it. You're not a boss. You're somebody's dogsbody. The real boss, your boss, said, "Go. Fetch." You're fetching me. You're planning on picking me up and dropping me at your master's feet. Alive. Preferably for both of us. But, as it all breaks down, you're the disposable one. Yeah. So, how to get me to your master's feet alive? Oh, I bet you brought money, lots of money, enough cash to make me salivate, and, hopefully, follow you anywhere. Well, Mr. Dogsbody, let's see what happens when instead of taking the money or sending it back, I slip out to the backyard and bury it, bury it someplace so remote, so deep, it'll remain hidden for six hundred years.

THE SEIGE

From the full-length drama, *Gentleman's War*

By W. Colin McKay

NOTE*: The play* <u>Gentleman's War</u> *is set in South Africa, 1900, during the South African War (Boer War). The South African War pitted the British Army against the Dutch Boers in a battle for geo-political supremacy of South Africa. It also served as the catalyst for the decades-long rule of apartheid. COLONEL CLARK-HOWELLL is one of the main characters and is fashioned somewhat after Colonel Baden-Powell of Boy Scouts fame. While the story is fictional, it is loosely based on Colonel Baden-Powell's experience as a commander during the actual Boer blockade of Mafeking, South Africa.*

BACKGROUND: The British have occupied a town by the name of Graysmith, but in so doing find themselves surrounded by Boers. The commanding officer is a delicate colonel who sings and dances for the entertainment his troops and the town he governs. He praises his own ability as a scout and has a "special" relationship with one of his boys training to also be a scout. JEDEDIAH CARSON, an American reporter for a major San Francisco newspaper sent to observe the few Americans fighting for the Boers, is apprehended by British forces. The

British suspect that he may be a spy for the Boers. Jed is detained in Graysmith. The inhabitants of the occupied town are allowed to go about their daily business.
SETTING: COLONEL CLARK-HOWELL'S office.
SCENE: COLONEL CLARK-HOWELLL, who has a secret project of taking young boys and training them to be scouts, asks Jed for help in building his reputation.

CLARK-HOWELLL

Mr. Carson, would you like to write about the Siege of Graysmith. . . based upon my own notes? You are a rugged man, Mr. Carson. The British journalists are, unfortunately, more dainty in their habits. . . America is a robust country while England, God bless her, is no longer. After the war I hope to make money lecturing and writing. But money is scarce in England while in America it is plentiful. After this war, I will need money to spend on a special project. To garner that money, I must go to America. But I must have a "robust" reputation to succeed there, a reputation you can help me achieve.

You'd write about my rugged ability to hold back a ruthless and determined enemy. You'd make the Boers the *enemy*. The Boers are real. Good writing could make them even more real. You say yourself they drop the odd cannon shell or two. Well, good writing could make that one shell into a hundred shells, creating nights of terror, with the populace of Graysmith huddled together in fear with only me to protect them. . . It would be what you call "a thrilling exploit". The

British journalists have already laid the groundwork. You would build upon that groundwork, create a monument to one man's bravery and superior leadership, *my* "bravery and superior leadership." I understand the sole warrior, prevailing against great odds, is well admired by Americans. Oh, and you would also stress my skill as a scout and my nobility of character. "Thrilling exploits" are read by many. And the number of gullible readers who believe them is considerable, correct?

Mr. Carson, a great deal of money can be made by both. You, as the chronicler of the thrilling exploit entitled, *The Official Diary of the Siege of Graysmith*, and by me, as its hero, standing firm and brave against the savage Boer onslaught. Now then, dear sir, do you accept my offer?

WE WANTED IT – WE TOOK IT

From the full-length drama, *Fallujah*

By W. Colin McKay

BACKGROUND: The play takes place after the Battle of Fallujah, 2004.

SETTING: Bare stage, spotlight on SOLDIER.

SCENE: An experienced United States Army combat SOLDIER addresses the audience.

SOLDIER

You wanna hear the truth about Fallujah? The first time Bush, Rumsfeld, someone ordered us into Fallujah we weren't ready. I mean, we had been saying all along we needed more time before we could attack. Christ, Fallujah was a goddamn cesspool of insurgents. The town had a population about three hundred thousand. We needed to make sure we had a plan to let the good guys out and keep the bad guys in. We needed more time. But nobody listened and we got sent in anyway.

It was miserable, but we kicked ass and had that fucking garbage dump almost under control, and then we were pulled out because all the fucking press could talk about was fucking civilians being killed. Bush and company had been warned if we went in too soon there'd be a lot of civilians take it in the shorts. We were ordered in anyway. We went in and, sure enough, civilians began dropping like wet goat turds. You shoulda heard the press howl then! Faster than a rats ass, we got pulled out because all the big shots at home thought the press was making Bush and the boys look bad. They pulled us out! Stupid! We had the terrorists by the balls and were ready to cut them off, but we're called back. Well, hell, the terrorists start yapping about how they beat us. How they kicked *our* ass instead of the other way around. The press picks up on *that*.

So, the big shots see what a fucking mistake it was to let the insurgents and the fucking world think they beat us and, so, we get sent back in. Only this time the insurgents have convinced themselves they can beat us and they don't give up. They fight, hide, door to door, room to room. It was a fucking nightmare. But we took the place. We went through it like a hot knife through butter. But it was still harder than it should've been. I know that some people feel sorry for us having to fight for Fallujah. Don't. We wanted Fallujah! We wanted it bad. And we took it! *That's* the truth.

CHAPTER 3

SCENES FOR TWO PEOPLE

BEING HERE DOES THINGS TO YOU

From the full-length drama, *Fallujah*

By W. Colin McKay

BACKGROUND: BENNETT, a Corporal, US Army, during the War in Iraq, earned the reputation as being a loose cannon. AMES, Corporal, US Army, is a female soldier who has crossed Bennett, even having gone so far as to threaten to kill him. They both are hard core. They both love war, hate war. Both of them are one step away from losing it.

SETTING: BENNET, getting dressed in battle gear after having had illicit sex with an Army nurse, addresses the audience.

SCENE: As he speaks to the audience, AMES enters, in full battle gear. Unseen by him, she listens for a moment, then crosses to him as he speaks. She waits until she's addressed by him before fully stepping into his scene.

BENNETT

(To audience)

Well, anyway, this girl I had been fucking had just left and Ames came up. I mean, Ames had been watching the whole time. She came over and just stared at me. I kept waiting for the bullshit to come down.

(Turns to AMES)

Well?

AMES

I know that girl from my first tour. Believe it or not she was virgin when she came over here. Saving herself for her boyfriend back home. The way she said it made me laugh. I'm sorry now I did that.

BENNETT

So, what do you want? More of the same? My dick's worn out. Check with me later.

(BENNETT starts to leave)

AMES

I was virgin, too. Not like her. But still virgin.

BENNETT

Yeah? We're all virgin once.

AMES

I'd never killed anybody. Never even thought about it.

(BENNET stops, turns to AMES)

BENNETT

You go to all the trouble to find me 'cause you want to tell me that?

AMES

(ignoring question)

I stood over him, the first guy I killed, just staring at him, looking at his eyes, waiting for him to blink. But he never did. I stared at him for a while, threw up, and moved on. When I had lost my virginity in bed, I cried. But for this one, I threw up.

BENNETT

Don't worry. He didn't notice.

AMES

What about you?

BENNETT

Me? No. I didn't notice, either. I wasn't there.

AMES

(Ignoring his sarcasm)

What'd you do when you killed your first person?

BENNETT

I don't remember. It wasn't that big a deal.

(AMES studies him for a moment)

AMES

You look like shit.

BENNETT

Fuck you.

AMES

No, I mean you don't look good from where I am. There's something wrong with my eyes. You know how everything looks through a night scope? That's the way everything looks to me. All the time. For real.

BENNETT

All the time?

AMES

Yeah. All the goddamn time.

BENNETT

(ironically)

You ever think about having your eyes checked?

(Ames glances at Bennett, walks away a few steps. She stares out in space, turns toward him, smiles, turns away)

AMES

It's not my eyes. It's---It's being here. You know what I mean?

BENNETT

Yeah, I suppose. Being here does things to you. Sometimes... you know... it's that way with me, too.

AMES

Yeah? You see things like that?

BENNETT

Yeah.

AMES

(Long beat)

I'm sorry for the shit I've been handing you at camp.

BENNETT

What's this? More shit?

AMES

No. Honest. What I thought about you… was all wrong.

BENNETT

I'm not an asshole?

AMES

No. You're still an asshole. That doesn't mean you're not a good guy.

BENNETT

You know, I don't care what you think, right? Whatever you think, whatever anyone thinks, doesn't make any goddamn difference to me.

AMES

(long beat)

Are you married?

BENNETT

Once. Not now.

AMES

Me, neither.

BENNETT

I thought you had a hubby and a kid?

AMES

Another me. Not me now. Not anymore.

(AMES moves away from BENNETT. She studies the
space around them. She drops to her knees and runs
her hands along the ground. Then stands and faces
BENNETT)

BENNETT

So, why are you here? Did you want something?

AMES

I was looking around tonight. I mean, at everyone. I looked at them,
trying to figure out who was going to live, who was going to die.

(AMES lifts rifle, aims at BENNETT)

BENNETT

Outstanding. You decide I'm not an asshole, so now you hunt me down to kill me?

AMES

No. But maybe I should.

BENNETT

Hey, I thought you were easing off.

AMES

(she lowers rifle)

I didn't mean it badly. I meant it as, well, as maybe a mercy killing. You want to die, don't you?

BENNETT

I haven't given it much thought.

AMES

Bullshit. You think it about all the time. I know I do.

BENNETT

Look, Ames, I'm fucked up. Hell, everyone here is fucked up.

AMES

Except for a few. The war lovers. They like it.

BENNETT

They don't count. Frankly, you don't seem so bad off.

AMES

That's the point. We're probably like most of the other third and fourth timers here. We'd all rather die than keep killing people for no good reason. I mean, the Haji are doing what I'd do. If some other country invaded America, I'd head for the hills and pick'em off one by one. Just like they're doing over here.

BENNETT

No wonder you're suicidal. You can't think like that. You're here to do a job. Good or bad. That's your job. You start trying to make sense out of all this and you'll wind up in the loony bin.

AMES

Would you, please, kill me?

BENNETT

What?

AMES

I'm asking you to kill me.

BENNETT

Jesus, you have lost your mind.

AMES

I'll kill you in return.

BENNETT

What?

AMES

You kill me and I'll kill you.

BENNETT

Uh, how'll you kill me if you're dead?

AMES

I'll come back as a ghost and scare you to death.

BENNETT

Look, Ames ----

AMES

Leave it like this---When the time's right, I want you to kill me. Or, if the time is right for you first, I'll kill you.

BENNETT

Jesus ---

AMES

I can't leave Iraq alive. Neither can you.

(They both recognize the truth of that statement,
BENNETT turns angrily away, then stops, faces
AMES and nods)

BENNETT

How --- How'll we know when the time's right?

AMES

We'll know.

BENNETT

Look, Ames, ---

AMES

You don't want to go home. You know that, don't you?

BENNETT

Yeah.

AMES

So, what happens if you don't get killed? Will you kill yourself?

BENNETT

Probably not. I don't have the balls to do it.

AMES

Same here. I want to, but I'm afraid and I don't know why.

BENNETT

Because despite all this talk, we don't really want to die.

AMES

Bullshit. If I stay alive what'll happen to me? I'll go home, divorce my husband, break my child's heart. She'll hate me. What'll I do? Goddamn it, what will I do? All I know how to do, really know how to do is fuck and kill.

BENNETT

Can't cook, huh?

AMES

(AMES breaks out laughing)

I bet that before Iraq you were simply a good guy.

BENNETT

I don't remember.

AMES

Maybe that's just as well.

BENNETT

You know the hardest thing for me to remember?

AMES

What?

BENNETT

When to stop killing.

AMES

I can't remember how to do anything else.

BENNETT

You said you also knew how to fuck.

AMES

That's a form of killing, right? I mean, over here? Like you and that girl?

BENNETT

Yeah. You put it that way. I guess so.

AMES

Do we have a deal?

BENNETT

Okay. Yeah. Maybe. We're getting ready to go back into Fallujah. Maybe everything'll take care of itself there. If not, well----we'll talk.

(AMES steps over to BENNETT, kisses him on the cheek)

AMES

We've already talked.

PLEASE STAY

From the novel, *One Hell of a Year*
By W. Colin McKay

BACKGROUND: ETHAN is a 16 year-old youth that has been mostly left alone to parent himself. His mother leaves him alone, going to stay with her boyfriend whenever his military father is overseas, which is quite often as he keeps re-enlisting. Bereft of parents, ETHAN'S go-to resource is Google which serves as his parent whenever he has a question about what to do and how to do it. He has found a companion, similarly abandoned, in EMMA, another 16 year-old who is also finding her way through the death of her mother and a preoccupied father.

SCENE: ETHAN has been telling EMMA of his carefully planned, detailed scenario for running away to Bakersfield, California and staying hidden until he turns eighteen.

EMMA

I wish you wouldn't.

ETHAN

What?

EMMA

I wish you wouldn't go.

ETHAN

I didn't mean right now. It'll take a couple of days to get tickets and plan where to stay. Last time I checked the youth hostels were booked, but it's scorching over there now. My guess, most of the kids in the hostels left and headed to the L.A. beaches.

EMMA

I knew what you meant. I meant, don't go at all.

ETHAN

I know it's a desert town, but Bakersfield is the place. I'll Facetime you as soon as I'm set.

EMMA

Ethan, shut up. You're missing the point, Ethan.

ETHAN

What point?

EMMA

Please, don't run away.

ETHAN

You mean, you don't want me to run away, at all?

EMMA

Yes.

ETHAN

You don't want me to run away, at all? You're asking me to stay?

EMMA

Yes.

ETHAN

You're asking me not to leave ever?

EMMA

Awkward phrasing, but, yes. What does it sound like I'm asking? You're so dumb sometimes I could puke.

ETHAN

Why?

EMMA

I would like you to be my boyfriend. If you'd be willing to have me be your girlfriend. We can't do that if you're in Bakersfield.

ETHAN

Could you say that again?

EMMA

We can't do that if you're in Bakersfield.

ETHAN

Uh, the other part.

EMMA

(pulls ETHAN to her, stares into his eyes)

I would like you as my boyfriend. Would you like me as your girlfriend?

ETHAN

Yes.

EMMA

You're happy for us to be boyfriend and girlfriend?

(Ethan nods slightly)

Was that a 'yes?'

ETHAN

Yes.

EMMA

Yes. For real?

ETHAN

Oh, yes.

(They kiss)

LOVE THEM DIFFERENT

From the full-length screenplay, *Twice Dead*

By W. Colin McKay

BACKGROUND: KIRK is investigating his brother's murder. He's talking to ELAINE, his slain brother's wife. KIRK has put her in hiding, fearing whoever murdered his brother will come after her.

SCENE: Elaine is telling Kirk about dealing with the pressure of hiding.

ELAINE

I'm glad I talked to the children. It was reassuring. But the little buggers...they're supposed to miss me.

> (smiles)

I guess all kids love staying with their Grammy. I did. God, they sounded so little. So innocent.

> (when Kirk doesn't answer she hesitates, then goes to
> him and puts her arm around him, and kisses him lightly
> on the cheek.)

What are you thinking about?

KIRK

That nun. She...reminded me of Mom. She seemed genuinely concerned about a stranger's welfare. Mom would've been like that. She liked everyone.

ELAINE

And your Dad?

KIRK

A big drunk Irishman cop whose cock was bigger than his brain.

ELAINE

Did your mom know?

KIRK

I don't know. I don't think so. I didn't have the heart to tell her. I just couldn't.

ELAINE

Did you ever tell that to your brother?

KIRK

He couldn't understand how I could've let a stranger tell her. He thought I was cruel. Thought I loved Dad more than Mom.

ELAINE

Did you?

KIRK

No, Loved them different. Dad was fun, a good time, the kind of guy that'd take you to ball games. You couldn't talk to him about problems. His answer to everything was to get drunk and raise hell. Mom, you'd talk to and she'd listen. Cry with you, if you needed. Then ... somehow she'd say something to make you feel better.

ELAINE

Your brother always complained that he couldn't talk to me. He was right, I guess. It scared me when he got worried about things. He was supposed to be. . . tough. And when he wasn't? I guess I'm like your father. Things didn't go right, I'd get drunk. . . and fantasize going to bed with his brother.

KIRK

Wait a minute.

ELAINE

(pressing on)

The first time I met you, I was impressed. You were a good looking guy. Just right for fantasies.

(beat)

You still are.

(she sees his discomfort)

I'm sorry. I've embarrassed you.

KIRK

Just a little. I'll live.

ELAINE

Do you ever have fantasies?

KIRK

Everybody does.

ELAINE

What are yours about?

KIRK

(pause)

You.

BRING THE MONEY

From the Original Screenplay, *Sea Witch*

By W. Colin McKay

BACKGROUND: ELLIDA WAGNER is set to inherit a large sum of money. All she must do is wait one week in a small sea town. She's afraid to wait because she's fears a psychopath who killed her first husband and raped her. She fled from him, but he was never caught. She's afraid he will be the one bringing the money and that he's coming to take her away. Her husband, Dave, knows nothing about her past. She's afraid to tell her husband the truth because of his jealousy.
SCENE: ELLIDA and DAVE are arguing about the money.

ELLIDA

Dave! Stop it! I don't know who would be bringing me the money. I don't care. I don't even want the money. Think about me, about me, for once.

DAVE

And what about me? I find out that my wife has come back to a town where it's public news she was raped, she walked around naked

ELLIDA

I didn't walk around. I was running. For my life. I had been beaten and raped. I was hurt. Didn't know where I was. I was running.

DAVE

With no clothes on. Where everyone saw your body. Your tits hanging out. Everything on display. Hurt or not, damn it, it's embarrassing to me. How many guys saw you? Three, four, a dozen. A goddamn dozen or so, gawking at my naked wife.

ELLIDA

Nobody gawked. I was covered in blood. I had cuts and scrapes all over my body. Nobody gawked!

DAVE

Sure. Then tell me who's that money from? A boyfriend? A former lover? Some guy you met afterwards who saw how good you looked naked and wanted a romp in the woods, too.

ELLIDA

What...what are you talking about?

DAVE

Nobody just leaves someone eight hundred thousand dollars! It was a lover, right? Some guy you were having an affair with here, while you were still married. That's why your husband beat you. You drove him to it! You...

ELLIDA

(screaming)

Stop it!

(pauses, stares at him)

Damn you. I hate you.

(She whirls to run away! He grabs her, hard. Ellida spins, slaps his face! He responds in a fury, clenches his fist to strike her, but she kicks out catching him square in the knee, buckling it. With a cry of pain, he falls. Ellida crosses to him, stares down at him as he moans, then stands straight)

Don't ever try to hit me again. . . Ever.

FIRST TIME

From the novel, *One Hell of a Year*
By W. Colin McKay

BACKGROUND: ETHAN is a 16 year-old youth mostly left alone to parent himself. His mother leaves to stay with her boyfriend whenever his military father is overseas, which is quite often as he keeps re-enlisting. As a convenience ETHAN'S go-to resource is the Google which serves as his parent whenever he has a question about what to do and how to do it. He has found a companion, similarly abandoned, in EMMA, another 16 year old who is also finding her way through the death of her mother and a preoccupied father.

SCENE: While EMMA regularly comes over to ETHAN'S house to talk or "mess around," she usually leaves at a regular time. This time she's stayed later than usual.

EMMA

May I stay with you tonight?

ETHAN

With me?

EMMA

Yes. You.

(Ethan freezes)

Ethan, what's wrong? Ethan? Passing out isn't necessary. All you have to do is tell me 'No.'

(Ethan takes EMMA in his arms and kisses her)

ETHAN

Emma, you taste like chocolate.

EMMA

Is that good or bad?

ETHAN

Good. Very good.

EMMA

Wanna another taste?

(they kiss)

ETHAN

Emma, I don't want to tell you 'no.'

EMMA

What do you want to tell me?

(ETHAN freezes again)

I love watching you think. Your face does all kinds of things. It really is sweet.

ETHAN

Hey, there's gotta be more. What about when I kiss you? Am I sweet then?

EMMA

Oh sure. That, too. But mostly it's when you're searching for something, trying to find the right answer. That's sweet.

(she giggles)

ETHAN

And that makes you giggle?

EMMA

I always giggle when I'm nervous.

ETHAN

(long beat)

Emma, would you like to sleep with me tonight?

EMMA

Yes. That's what I thought we'd do.

ETHAN

Uh, I mean . . . uh . . . would you like to have sex with me tonight?

EMMA

That's what I thought we were going to do.

ETHAN

Uh, you did?

EMMA

You're supposed to be pretty smart. Are you sure they measured your I.Q. correctly?

ETHAN

I don't have rubbers. I mean, condoms. I mean…

EMMA

Oh.

ETHAN

Oh? Uh, are you on the pill?

EMMA

I bought these condoms on the way over.

(She holds out a package of condoms)

ETHAN

God. Was it embarrassing?

EMMA

It embarrassed the boy who sold them to me more than it embarrassed me.

(ETHAN fiddles with package, then blurts out --)

ETHAN

I don't know how to use a condom.

EMMA

You don't?

ETHAN

Do you?

EMMA

Oh, goodness, no.

ETHAN

Let me Google "How To Make Love To A Virgin."

(EMMA looks around as ETHAN goes to the computer)

EMMA

I want to remember this room forever. I never really noticed the color of your walls before. Amber. It makes the room feel warm. I like amber.

(ETHAN types on the keyboard muttering aloud as he does)

ETHAN

"How to make love to a virgin." Yes!

(he sits back, EMMA leans in and looks at screen)

EMMA

Wow! There are a lot of sites.

(ETHAN studies the screen for a moment and clicks on site, they both lean in closer, read, then after a moment, they sit back)

ETHAN

I guess we should talk about fear.

EMMA

Okay.

ETHAN

Emma, are you afraid?

EMMA

At first, I thought I might be, but, surprisingly, I guess, no, I'm not. Are you?

ETHAN

When we first started talking about it, I was. A little. But, now, no. I'm not afraid, either.

> (they lean back in to the computer, continue
> reading, they are closer together than before. After
> a moment, they lean back, pause before speaking)

How to use a rubber was pretty clear.

EMMA

I'll never look at a banana the same again.

ETHAN

Whenever you hear anyone order a banana split, think of me.

> (they laugh, read some more)

EMMA

Being ready is important. Do you think you're ready, Ethan? I think I am.

ETHAN

I. . . don't know. I want sex, with you, but, well, all the stuff we read says being ready to have sex isn't the same as being ready to make love.

EMMA

I think it's sweet that you take this much time because I'm a virgin.

ETHAN

For you? Uh, thanks, but. . . well, it's for me, too. I'm virgin.

(Emma kisses him, then continues reading)

Look, it says, the perfect gentleman spreads rose petals on the bed. Damn. I don't have any flowers. I can run next door and pick some from Mrs. Wilson's garden. She'd never know.

EMMA

(laughing)

No, it's fine. Besides I'm afraid that once you ran outside you'd keep running and not come back.

ETHAN

(serious)

I'd come back. I'll never run away from you.

EMMA

Do you love me, Ethan?

ETHAN

(softly, barely above whisper)

Yes.

EMMA

Ethan, I know you love me, but you have to say so for it to count--

ETHAN

(ironically)

Uh, will it 'count' if I cross my fingers?

EMMA

Oh no. For it to count you have to say it without your fingers crossed.

ETHAN

(serious)

With my fingers un-crossed, I love you. And will stay with you as long as long you'll let me.

EMMA

I love you, too.

ETHAN

What music do you want? The site said first-time intercourse should have music in the background.

EMMA

Christmas music.

(ETHAN clicks on the computer and Christmas music

fills the stage)

ETHAN

I want to make you happy.

(He goes to her. They embrace)

EMMA

Emma, are you sure you're ready?

EMMA

Ready for what? You have to say it.

ETHAN

(pauses)

To lose your virginity.

EMMA

Ethan, are you ready to lose you virginity?

ETHAN

Yes.

EMMA

One thing.

ETHAN

What?

EMMA

When do we use the banana?

(They chuckle, grow serious embrace)

ETHAN

Are you ready?

EMMA

Yes. Are you ready?

ETHAN

Yes.

EMMA

The ayes have it. It's unanimous. We'll both make love for the first time.

ETHAN

It's unanimous, we'll both make love to a virgin.

(they embrace and kiss)

ANY WAY YOU CAN

From the full-length drama, *Children of Shame*
By W. Colin McKay

BACKGROUND: During the Bosnia-Serbia conflict, MOLLY HINSON is working as a contract investigator for the U.N. Council for War Crimes. Her boss, CAPTAIN FRANK MORGAN, USN, wants her to interview a Christian missionary who works in the middle of Bosnia. MOLLY wanted to go home on leave but he talked her into staying for the one investigation. The major problem is that the missionary in question is a General in the Christian Missionary Army, and MOLLY despises missionaries in general but specifically the Christian Missionary Army.

SCENE: A Brigadier General in the Christian Missionary Army supposedly has photographic evidence of war crimes committed by a high-ranking member of the Serbian Army. The War Crimes Tribunal has been investigating this Serbian with no success. FRANK wants MOLLY to find the damning photographic evidence.

FRANK

I know the real Molly Hinson. She hates man's inhumanity to man. Help me find those women. ✳

MOLLY

I have other plans. Sorry.

FRANK

This might be our best chance to bring Jovanovich to trial. ✳

MOLLY

Come on, Frank. I need time off. Find someone else.

FRANK

There is no one else.

MOLLY

Christ.

(hesitates)

If I say okay—and I'm not saying I am--what's the set-up?✳

FRANK

I'll make up a name of some sub-sub agency and put in a request to investigate the CMA. Make sure they're following the mandate.

MOLLY

What mandate is that?

FRANK

I haven't created one yet. But don't worry, it'll sound real.

MOLLY

Oh, great.

FRANK

I'll sign my name approving the investigation. It'll get you in.

MOLLY

No way. They'd spot the scam off the top and that'd be that, plus big trouble for me, not figuring the pile of crap waiting for you.

FRANK

These are civilians. Missionaries. They'll get the papers the same day you arrive. They'll buy it.

MOLLY

You're so sure?

FRANK

I'm sure.

MOLLY

And, if they don't, you'll tell the U.N. you made me do it and go to jail for me, right?

FRANK

Molly, nothing'll happen. You'll be in and out.

MOLLY

You really want this guy, don't you?

FRANK

Yes, I do.

MOLLY

It's a good thing for you I think you're cute.

FRANK

What's that got to do with anything? ✳

MOLLY

You'll find out. Okay, I'm in the mission. On my own. Now what?

FRANK

Get them out anyway you can. I'll get them to a group who'll take it from there. Will you do it?

MOLLY

Where's the mission?

FRANK

Serbia.

MOLLY

Oh, Christ.

FRANK

On the border. Just inside. It's not like it's in the middle of the damn country.

MOLLY

Which border?

FRANK

Bosnia.

MOLLY

What the hell? C'mon, Frank. You trying to get me killed?

FRANK

I'll be waiting for them. You get them to me, I'll do the rest.

(MOLLY stares at FRANK in mock dismay, then nods her head)

MOLLY

Okay. Okay. I'll do it. That 'man's inhumanity to man' stuff gets me every time.

FRANK

Thanks.

MOLLY

I want more than a 'thanks.' ✳

FRANK

What then? Name it.

MOLLY

(goes to him, puts her arms round him)

I want you. . . tonight.

FRANK

Uh, what would I tell my wife?

MOLLY

That's your problem.

(FRANK hesitates, clearly caught in a dilemma. MOLLY
runs her hand down a very uncomfortable FRANK'S
chest, hesitates, smiles, shakes her head)

Skip it. I just wanted to see how far you'd go for your commitment
against inhumanity in the world. I'll settle for an expensive dinner when
I get back. . . if I get back.

FRANK

Thank you.

(goes to her)

See you tomorrow. . . give you all the details. And. . . once more. . .
thanks.

MOLLY

For taking the job or letting you go?

FRANK

Both.

MOLLY

Yeah. Now get the hell out of here.

(FRANK starts to leave)

One thing. I'll do my best to be a good girl. But I must warn you. I can only listen so long to someone hand me sanctimonious crap before I puke all over them.

FRANK

Have them send me the cleaning bill

BURN IT DOWN

From the one-act comedy, *Burning Issue*

By W. Colin McKay

BACKGROUND: **FRANKLIN HOLLY** is trying to convince **ELLEN WILSON** to burn down her bankrupt bookstore and collect the insurance money.

SETTING: **FRANKLIN** has entered **ELLEN'S** empty bookstore. All books and other items are gone, auctioned or sold at a loss.

SCENE: He finds a lone book apparently overlooked during the bankruptcy sale.

FRANKLIN

(Calling out)

Anybody here!

(Waits a second, calls again)

I want to buy this book.

(Again waits, gets no answer, calls out)

I'm pretty sure you're here.

ELLEN (off stage)

I'll be right there.

(We HEAR a Toilet flush. After a moment, ELLEN walks out, straightening her clothes)

We're closed.

FRANKLIN

I want to buy this book.

ELLEN

I heard you. It's not for sale and, even if it were, we're closed.

FRANKLIN

When do you open?

(ELLEN looks at him incredulously, then)

ELLEN

Sir, does this look like a store that's ever going to open again?

FRANKLIN

I was here last year. You were open then.

ELLEN

Do you see any difference between the store then and what you see now?

FRANKLIN

You had more books?

ELLEN

Right. Do you see any books in the store now?

FRANKLIN

(Holds up the small book)

This one.

ELLEN

(ELLEN reaches over, takes it back)

It's not for sale. Do you see any others?

FRANKLIN

No?

ELLEN

Correct. There are no more books in the store.

FRANKLIN

You sold them all?

ELLEN

If you want to call it that. We returned what we could and practically gave away the others. Do you know what that means?

FRANKLIN

What?

ELLEN

We're closed. . . forever.

FRANKLIN

I don't believe you.

ELLEN

Well, that may be, but that doesn't change the fact that I am out of business.

FRANKLIN

What happened?

ELLEN

The discount chain store three blocks down. We were a local business who gave better service, were familiar with the stock, and had a sense of what kind of book fit what kind of person. The discount chain did none of that, but gave lower prices. They're still in business.

FRANKLIN

No customer loyalty?

ELLEN

Long time ago. When I was growing up. But the neighborhood's changed. Times have changed.

FRANKLIN

Maybe you should just burn the store down and use the insurance money to start again in a new bookstore where there are more loyal customers.

ELLEN

Burn the store down?

FRANKLIN

An idea?

ELLEN

That's it! Sir, we're closed. I thought I had locked the front door. Obviously, that was not the case. I apologize. But we are closed!

FRANKLIN

It wasn't my fault. The front door. I found it unlocked.

ELLEN

I didn't say it was your fault. I just said. . . Well, it should've been.

FRANKLIN

I found it unlocked.

ELLEN

I know that. I'm just saying that it. . .

(Takes a beat)

I'm just saying that it's time for you to go. I mean it. Goodbye, sir.

FRANKLIN

All right.

(turns to go, stops, turns back)

You're not staying in the store overnight, are you?

SCREEN LOVE

From the one-act play, *Chatterbox*

By W. Colin McKay

BACKGROUND: JIM has found MELISSA online after a long period of time. At one time, they were lovers. Both are married to other people. They are communicating through Instant Messaging. Whenever they instant message each other they pantomime typing. The "typing" is to be suggested. There should not be any attempt at reality. The dialog should be well-paced, not hesitant as if reading from a computer. Whenever they are away from the computers they are talking to themselves.

SETTING: The stage is bare except for two computers on each side of the stage, facing each other.

SCENE: JIM and MELISSA, middle-aged, sitting at their computers. Jim wants to talk about their love affair, but Melissa resists doing so.

JIM

Can I talk about dancing, then?

MELISSA

I guess so.

JIM

You were a great dancer.

MELISSA

Thank you. So were you.

JIM

I loved dancing with you.

MELISSA

Careful, where you're headed.

JIM

Everyone enjoyed watching us dance. Is that okay?

MELISSA

Yes. They certainly loved watching us.

JIM

Mostly they enjoyed watching you. Especially when doing the Tango. Boy, did you steam up the dance floor. Whoops. Is that okay to say?

MELISSA

Yes, I guess it's okay. Just be --

JIM

Our bodies were one. Remember? Your breasts against me.

MELISSA

That's not –

JIM

Your legs stretching out and slinking across the floor.

> (Hesitant, MELISSA rises from her chair, careful at first, yet drawn by the moment. JIM rises from his computer moves toward her)

We'd sweep across the floor, my hands barely touching your breasts with each partial turn.

> (MELISSA runs to him and THEY begin dancing, not quite touching. They never touch. JIM doesn't speak directly to her, but she does acknowledge him with longing and desire. As if MELISSA can hear JIM in her mind)

At the end, I'd dip you with a flourish --

> (They dip)

We'd hold. Your smoldering look destroying me!

(They hold)

And then! I'd pull you up to a deep kiss!

(They pose a deep kiss)

We would hold the kiss. So much in love.

>(MELISSA hurries back to her side of the stage, embarrassed, fighting tears. She sits at her computer. JIM hurries back to his computer)

Do you remember?

MELISSA

Of course, I do.

>(MELISSA pauses begins to cry, stops, slowly recovers)

But…we can't talk about it.

JIM

Can we Skype? At least Facetime?

MELISSA

No.

JIM

I want to see you.

MELISSA

No. Don't ask anymore. Please.

JIM

Okay.

> (Confused, JIM fidgets with his computer. He rises and walks away from it. Abruptly, he hurries back and begins typing)

I remember when we made love for the first time, your touch was so gentle and tender. Different from the passionate touching of the Tango, but much more passionate in it's truth. You loved me as much as I loved you.

> (MELISSA sits still at her computer, fighting back tears. JIM begins typing with great passion)

I have so much to say to you. So much.

MELISSA

That may be, my darling. But, please understand. I can't allow you to say it.

WHERE TO BELONG

From the full-length drama, *Nagasaki Dust*
By W. Colin McKay

NOTE: *Based upon a true story.*

BACKGROUND: JOHN OKUI, a Japanese-American, visited Japan as World War Two broke out and he was captured by the Japanese, conscripted in the Imperial Army. After the war, he is tried for treason by the United States Army.

SETTING: A dance at UCLA.

SCENE: MARIKO ONO, John Okui's girlfriend, also, Japanese-American. They're students at UCLA and a fellow student, a white girl, used a racial slur referencing Mariko as Chinese. One of John's friend's became angry and defended Mariko, while John remained silent.

MARIKO

I think he's more upset than I am. And I'm pretty angry.

JOHN

You made that clear.

(MARIKO stares hard at JOHN. He says nothing. The MUSIC begins and THEY take hands, ready to begin dancing again. It's a slow dance)

MARIKO

John?

JOHN

Yeah?

MARIKO

Why didn't you tell that girl to shut up? Why did you leave it up to him?

JOHN

She was with Pete. I mean, it would've been rude to. . . well. . .

MARIKO

She was being rude to me. Do you think any of the other boys there would've put up with me being rude to their girl friends?

JOHN

What are you getting at, Mari?

MARIKO

It hurt my feelings when you didn't stand up for me.
(stops dancing)

If she had been rude to you, I would've scratched her eyes out. Don't you get tired of the name-calling?

JOHN

Sure, I do.

MARIKO

Then say something when it happens.

JOHN

You don't.

MARIKO

Yes, I do. . . when I'm with friends. But. . . not when I'm with you.

JOHN

But why?

MARIKO

It would embarrass me to have people see you were afraid to speak up for yourself.

(JOHN is speechless, stunned by the response. Then--)

JOHN

Damn it, Mari, who are we? Are we Americans? Americans of Japanese Ancestry? Japanese who live in America. . .

MARIKO

(cutting him off)

We're simply John and Mariko.

JOHN

No. We have to belong somewhere.

MARIKO

Belonging to each other isn't enough?

JOHN

No!

WILL I SHAME YOU?

From the full-length drama, *Gentleman's War*
By W. Colin McKay

NOTE: *The play* <u>Gentleman's War</u> *is set in South Africa, 1900, during the South African War (Boer War). The South African War pitted the British Army against the Dutch Boers in a battle for geo-political supremacy of South Africa. It also served as the catalyst for the decades-long rule of Apartheid. COLONEL CLARK-HOWELLL is one of the main characters and is fashioned somewhat after Colonel Baden-Powell of Boy Scout fame. While the story is fictional, it is loosely based on Colonel Baden-Powell's experience as a commander during the actual Boer blockade of Mafeking, South Africa.*

BACKGROUND: The British have occupied a town by the name of Graysmith, but in so doing find themselves surrounded by Boers. The commanding officer is a delicate Colonel who sings and dances for the entertainment his troops and the town he governs. He praises his own ability as a scout and has a "special" relationship with one of his boys training to also be a scout. JEDEDIAH CARSON, an American reporter for a major San Francisco newspaper sent to observe the few Americans fighting for the Boers, is apprehended by British forces. The British suspect that he may be a spy for the Boers. Jed is detained in Graysmith, the town occupied by the British. However, the town is surrounded by Boers. The inhabitants of the occupied town are allowed to go about their daily business. One of the inhabitants is the widow, KATIE McKINNON, an East Indian who had been married to a British officer killed early in the conflict. She now runs a boarding house in Graysmith. During the period of his confinement, JEDIDIAH is housed at KATIE McKINNON's boarding house. They are drawn to each other.

SETTING: KATIE's house

SCENE: KATIE and JED have had sex for the first time.

KATIE

Have there been many other women?

JED

Some.

KATIE

Did you love them?

JED

Some. But. . . none of them like I love you.

KATIE

Jedediah, after we leave Graysmith. . . if you become ashamed of me don't lie to me. Tell me. I'd return home. I'd rather be alone without you, than ever shame you by my presence.

JED

Is that what happened with your husband?

KATIE

He meant well . . .

JED

If you don't want to tell me, you don't have to.

KATIE

(nods, but goes ahead)

When we left India, he became aware I was. . . not white. I tried. But I am not a British wife.

JED

Nor should you be, damn it. You're no white lily moaning in stretched A's about the weight of a dew drop on your pinky. You're a woman.

KATIE

He was ashamed of me.

JED

I'll never become ashamed of you and I'll kick the living hell out of the first man who says one word against you. Christ, I'm the one who should be worrying about you becoming ashamed of me.

(KATIE moves to speak. He quiets her again)

Look, Katie, we've never talked about it, but I want you to know. I've done things. . . bad things. And some of the people I dallied with were pretty bad, too. The women included. I don't apologize for it. Hell, for the most part, I liked it. Except for once. . . But, hell, that's over and, well, after meeting you, I don't intend to go back to my old life. After I'm through here, I plan to change. Be a better man. I want you to know that.

KATIE

You're a good man now, Jedediah.

JED

Not good enough for you. I know it. You're the. . . most beautiful. . . good woman I've ever known. And I intend on trying to get better. . . for you.

KATIE

Now, it's your turn to make me smile. All my husband could do was to demand that I improve.

JED

He must've been a goddamn idiot.

KATIE

He was British.

JED

That explains it.

(THEY kiss again. JED lifts her up in his arms)

And damned if you're not the best woman I've ever had under the blankets.

(KATIE laughs as the LIGHTS go out)

GAZING INTO THE HORIZON

From the one-act comedy, *Horizon*

By W. Colin McKay

BACKGROUND: KIRK and ALISON are engaged.

SETTING: Kirk and Alison are together at the beach. General food stuffs for a picnic lie about. There is a small spat occurring.

SCENE: At this moment, KIRK is staring out into space, away from ALISON. They argue in silences.

KIRK

We have now come full circle in our little drama. I've already told you that I'm--

(KIRK stops speaking)

ALISON

You stopped mid-sentence.

KIRK

Yes.

ALISON

Because you suddenly realized I didn't ask, as I asked before, what you were *thinking about*, but, instead, I changed and asked what you *saw* when you stared out at the horizon?

(before KIRK can answer)

And if you say, 'I see the horizon' I'll jump off this cliff right now.

KIRK

Well…

ALISON

I mean it.

KIRK

How far down is it?

ALISON

Not funny.

KIRK

Sorry.

(Beat)

When I look out into the horizon, it's not what I think or see.

ALISON

Then?

KIRK

It's what I hear.

ALISON

And?

KIRK

They say sound never dies. Like space itself, sound is perpetual. Lack of volume doesn't constitute death. From moment of the impact which produced it, that one single sound wave becomes infinite. It keeps echoing through the universe until it gradually merges with another sound which, in turn, will merge with another sound, and so forth, and so on.

ALISON

Sound's existence is eternal.

KIRK

Yes.

ALISON

(icy)

I've <u>heard</u> all that before.

KIRK

Irony always impresses me.

ALISON

You're moving off point.

KIRK

I am?

ALISON

I asked what you saw when you stared at the horizon. You responded by saying it wasn't so much about what you saw but what you heard. You then went on to explain, as to a child, how sound never dies. Ignoring the intentional, or not, insult, ignoring your praise of ironical comments, I am still waiting for you to tell me what sounds you hear when staring at the horizon.

KIRK

Oh.

ALISON

Precisely.

KIRK

I see.

ALISON

Very funny. Please, tell me what you hear coming from the horizon.

KIRK

Well, my love, what I hear are not sounds emanating from the horizon, but sounds bouncing along the ocean, off the waves, into the horizon.

ALISON

(pause)

Away?

KIRK

(pause as Alison waits)

Yes.

ALISON

"Into?"

KIRK

Sadly, yes again.

ALISON

(she waits for him to elaborate, he doesn't)

What kind of sounds?

KIRK

Past sounds?

(ALISON shakes her head, turns her back on KIRK)

ALISON

Oh God, is this going to be one of your off-the-wall moments? If so, I refuse to listen.

KIRK

I didn't know I had off-the-wall moments.

ALISON

Incessantly.

KIRK

Off the wall?

ALISON

Off the wall. Bouncing back and forth.

KIRK

Funny. You'd think I'd be bruised from all the bouncing.

(ALISON turns angrily back to him)

ALISON

No! I am the one who is bruised. Now, damn it, what do you hear?

KIRK

Into the horizon or off the bouncing wall?

ALISON

Goddamn it!

KIRK

I take that as 'horizon.' Very well, I'll tell you what I hear. But you need to prepare to hear it.

(ALISON takes out a picnic chair and sits)

Comfy?

(Sees her nod)

Excellent.

(draws himself up to speak)

I hear laughter. Oh, there's some anger. Some passionate love-making. But, mostly, there is laughter. Light. Tinkly.

ALISON

That's it?

KIRK

That's it. I have difficulty with higher pitches.

ALISON

I don't understand.

KIRK

Neither do I.

ALISON

What do you mean 'Neither do I?' You're the one listening to it. You should understand what you hear.

KIRK

Oh, I misunderstood what I was to understand.

(beat)

Yes, I definitely understand what I hear. But it's confusing.

ALISON

In what way?

KIRK

The only way I hear laughter anymore is when I stare out to the horizon and listen.

ALISON

The only way?

KIRK

I don't understand why that would be.

(pause)

Do you?

(ALISON rises, closes the seat, picks up the picnic basket, starts to leave, then turns around, and walks back to him. KIRK hasn't moved. ALISON puts the basket down)

ALISON

I'll call for a ride. I'll leave the basket. I'm not hungry.

(ALISON takes out her cell phone and exits with purpose)

(After she exits, Kirk stands there for a few moments, stares out, starts to laugh, suddenly stops. He picks up the closed chair, opens it, sits, reaches into the picnic basket left behind, pulls out a sandwich and begins to eat. As he chews in contentment, he closes his eyes)

LATE LETTER

From the one-act play, *Tables*

By W. Colin McKay

BACKGROUND: "TABLES" is a one-act comedy serially connected by separate scenes, each following from the other.

SETTING: Outside a bus terminal. There's the sound of buses.

SCENE: MARK and HELEN are an elderly couple who have found each other again after several years and now are parting, for only a brief time. They enter. Mark is carrying a suitcase. Helen carries a small basket. They stop. He puts the suitcase down for a moment.

MARK

Nothing's in it that wasn't in it when I came, but it seems heavier leaving.

HELEN

You will come back next week?

MARK

I promise. I'll call every night I'm away.

HELEN

Call after I'm in bed. We can talk dirty for awhile.

MARK

Helen, it's a damn good thing I came looking for you. If you had been left alone for much longer no man within a fifty-yard radius of you would've been safe.

HELEN

Fifty-foot.

MARK

After I get back, I'll never be further away than this.

(he kisses her)

God, how I love kissing you.

(Mark gives Helen a hug that lifts her off the floor. She loses her breath for a moment, but still enjoys the hug and kiss)

HELEN

Oh, my. I'm afraid we may have enjoyed that hug too much.

(HELEN steps back, reaches into her coat and pulls out a wrapping of cloth napkins, puts them on top of the basket)

MARK

What's that?

HELEN

Nothing. It's a surprise for you when you open the basket on the train.

MARK

I can smell them from here. They're chocolates.

HELEN

They're squished chocolates. You hugged me too hard.

MARK

I love squished chocolates. Especially ones I squished hugging you. I'll eat one before the train leaves.

(MARK reaches for the cloth wrapping, but HELEN
pulls the basket away)

HELEN

No! Open them later. You'll like them better when you're hungry.

MARK

Are you kidding? I'm always hungry for your chocolates. Let me have at least one before I get on.

(He takes the basket, puts it down and opens cloth
wrapping. He hesitates and in surprise, reaches in and

pulls out a letter)

This doesn't look too good.

(forced playful)

You're not telling me about a secret husband?

HELEN

Of course not.

MARK

About how much you're going to miss me?

(Mark starts to open it, Helen reaches out and stops him.
Mark looks at her, questioning)

HELEN

Please wait. Read it on the train. Please. . . I. . . I don't want to be here
when you read it.

MARK

Why not now?

(HELEN briefly considers, then nods toward MARK)

HELEN

You can read it now, if you want.

(MARK opens the letter and begins reading aloud)

MARK

"Dear, Mark. . . "

HELEN

Not aloud.

MARK

(ignoring her)

"Two hours ago, I watched you walk away from me. I sat in the restaurant, looking out the window and watched you walk away and I knew I'd never see you again.

(looks up at her, then continues)

"I knew the great love of my life was gone forever and had taken all happiness with him. I wanted to take back what I had said. But I didn't know how. I simply didn't know how to do it. I'm trying now. I love you and want to spend the rest of my life with you. . . "

(MARK looks up at her again)

When did you write this?

HELEN

Forty years ago.

MARK

Why didn't you mail it?

HELEN

I did, but you moved away so quickly, it got returned with no forwarding address. Nobody knew where you had gone.

MARK

I wanted to hurt you. That was my mistake.

> (beat)

Thank God, you didn't leave.

IS THAT A "YES?"

From the novel, *One Hell of a Year*

By W. Colin McKay

BACKGROUND: ETHAN is a 16 year-old youth left alone to parent himself. His mother leaves him alone, going to stay with her boyfriend whenever his military father is overseas, which is quite often as he keeps re-enlisting. Bereft of parents, ETHAN'S go-to resource is the Google which serves as his parent whenever he has a question about what to do and how to do it. He has found a companion, similarly abandoned, in EMMA, another 16 year old who is also finding her way through the death of her mother and a preoccupied father.

SETTING: Bare stage

SCENE: ETHAN has asked EMMA why her father is so distant.

ETHAN

You don't have to tell me. It doesn't make any difference. I still want to be with you.

EMMA

Would you ever lie to me, Ethan?

ETHAN

No. I wouldn't.

EMMA

Even if your lies would protect me from something bad?

ETHAN

Like what?

EMMA

Like anything.

ETHAN

(thinks)

No. Not even if the lies would protect you from something bad.

EMMA

Promise?

ETHAN

Why?

EMMA

Because I want to know. Do you promise?

ETHAN

Promise.

EMMA

Really?

ETHAN

Damn it, Emma. I won't lie to you. First, it doesn't matter if I did, you could tell by looking at me. But, second, I don't want to. I promise. No lies. What's wrong, Emma?

EMMA

You asked once if my dad worried about me being here. I told you he doesn't care.

ETHAN

You said you didn't want to talk about it.

EMMA

I like you. You like me. We spend a great deal of time together...I'll tell you.

ETHAN

It's OK.

EMMA

(composes herself)

Mom died of pneumonia when I was eight. Daddy met my step-mom pretty soon and they got married. I didn't like her or her son. He was three years older than me. I tried to be a good daughter. Daddy says it wasn't long before he knew it was a bad marriage, but he kept hoping it would get better. So anyway, her son didn't like me at all. I was a hundred times smarter than he was. My shoe was smarter than he was. He'd punch me when nobody was around. He was big. Not like you. Not tall. But heavy. Really fat…He raped me. My step-mom and Daddy were shopping. I was nine. Daddy wanted to kill him. My step-mom blamed me, saying I seduced her son. They divorced. She and her son left to go live in Utah. We haven't heard from them since. Daddy and I went to counseling for a year. It helped me a lot. But not him.

(pauses then continues)

Daddy blames himself for what happened to me. It's made him. . . ashamed. I've gotten through it. I'm moving on. But the bad part is lately he doesn't like to be around me much. He's always been uncomfortable when I'm around, but lately he goes into his workroom, shuts the door, and refuses to even acknowledge I'm in the house.

ETHAN

No other family for you to go to? An Aunt? Grandmother?

EMMA

(shakes her head "no")

Oh, Ethan, I'm not like you. I don't like being by myself. I want a family. A real family. I used to have it before Mommy died.

ETHAN

You still have a dad.

EMMA

No. No, I don't. A real father talks to you, gives you advice. Notices you're there. My father hates me because I make him feel guilty. He avoids me. For me, it's terrible. I want to be part of a loving family. I had a dad. But, he's not there any more, and I'm afraid.

ETHAN

(non-believing)

I know it sounds dumb. But, I bet it'll all work out okay.

EMMA

Says who?

ABOUT THE AUTHOR

I knew without a doubt that I wanted to "be in theatre" from the time I was ten years old and lived across the street from the La Jolla Playhouse. I would sneak in the back door, not during performances mind you, but during rehearsals. I was fascinated how the actors could do all those different emotions and roles and then be willing to talk to me about what they were thinking. I watched the directors urging the actors to develop their characters and show them what to do on stage. It was magic, and it has informed the rest of my professional life.

The written word was always my go-to mode of expression, maybe because I was an only child and this was one of those activities that did not depend on others for full participation. I'm fortunate I was able to morph this ability into a career as a professional writer in the theatre. Just where I wanted to be.

Challenges, aside from making me tear my hair out, have honed my skills and taught me countless bits of wisdom to inform what I do and skills I use to ply my craft. This keeps me working on projects similar to this collection of monologues and scenes and drives me to seek out new endeavors, new challenges.

Along the way I have been supported and encouraged by many colleagues, friends and family. My life is richer and keeps me on task because of my wife, who is my primary cheerleader and hardest critic. My twin sons have loved me and taught me many life lessons, they are identical twins, but each has individually created a relationship with me that influences my every move. Thank you to all.

McKayisms

"I have heard that there is a direct correlation between memory and IQ."

"You can't be brilliant and afraid of failure."

"Risk is an adventure, not a threat."

"Uncontrolled fear produces controlled art."

"Failure is failing without knowing how or why or what to think about doing again."

"There's no problem with over-reaching. The problem is not reaching, at all."

"You don't have to memorize your lines. In fact, you don't have to be in this play."

Made in the USA
San Bernardino, CA
05 January 2019